Rx America

A Script for Survival

by

David Hayden

First published by AuthorHouse 04/13/04

ISBN: 1-4140-7058-6 (e-book)
ISBN: 1-4184-3306-3 (Paperback)

This book is printed on acid free paper.

INTRODUCTION TO RxAMERICA

MUCH HAS HAPPENED SINCE I COPYRIGHTED THIS BOOK IN 1996; SADLY, MOST OF THE EVENTS HAVE BEEN TRAGIC.

WE HAVE NOW REACHED, IN OUR HISTORY, A TIME OFTEN REFERRED TO AS THE "END GAME", OR "END OF DAYS", OR EVEN ARMAGEDDON.

THE EMOTIONALLY SHATTERING DEATHS ON SEPTEMBER 11, 2001 WERE CERTAINLY MORE THAN THE PROVERBIAL WAKE UP CALL; THE COWARDLY ATTACKS WARNED US AND THE REST OF THE WORLD THAT FOR THE FORESEEABLE FUTURE, THAT WAS THE WAY LIFE WOULD BE.

WE ALL FORM OUR LIFE'S OPINIONS BASED IN LARGE PART ON THE BEATINGS WE BEAR AND THE SMILES THAT WE SHARE. VERY FEW OF US ESCAPE UNSCATHED, ALTHOUGH THERE ARE THOSE WHO HAVEN'T A CLUE.

I DROWNED WHEN I WAS FIVE AND WAS DEAD FOR OVER AN HOUR. THAT OF COURSE EXPLAINS THE BRAIN DAMAGE BUT IS FAR SHY OF THE WHOLE STORY. MY TIME SPENT THAT HOUR DEFINED THE REMAINDER OF MY LIFE. DURING MY FOUR PLUS YEARS IN THE MARINE CORPS I WAS CERTAIN THAT I'D NEVER MAKE TWENTY YEARS OF AGE. THE NATURAL COURSE FOLLOWING MY DISCHARGE WAS TO FULLY IMMERSE MYSELF IN THE PSYCHEDELIC SIXTIES AND COLLEGE.

SUDDENLY I WAS THIRTY, LIVING IN LAHAINA, DIVORCED FROM MY WONDERFUL WIFE AND WINGING MY WAY THROUGH THE WORLD. AS GOOD FORTUNE WOULD HAVE IT I TURNED FORTY ON MAUI AND AS SURE AS BAD LUCK FOLLOWS GOOD, TURNED FIFTY BACK IN THE MAINLAND.

NOW A YEAR AWAY FROM SIXTY I AM GRATEFUL MORE THAN EVER FOR THE GUIDANCE GIVEN ME DURING THAT ONE HOUR IN MY FIFTH YEAR. WITH EACH VASECTOMY I APPLAUD MY DECISION TO HAVE NOT ADDED YET ANOTHER SOUL TO THE CENSUS.

I AM PERSONALLY CONTENT WITH MY TWO RUBBER MAID BOXES, MY GUITAR, MY GUNS, AND MY TOOLS; AND A SECOND AND THIRD DIVORCE. I HAVE BEEN SINCE THE AGE OF FIVE, SAD BEYOND DESCRIPTION REGARDING THE CONDUCT OF OUR SPECIES.

FOR MOST OF US, WE DO THE BEST WE CAN; FOR THOSE WHO WILL FOLLOW, WE MUST DO BETTER.

RxAmerica

A Script for Survival

Written by David Hayden

"The only mistake the Good Lord made regarding Mother Earth was when she provided free will to a species of animal that would utilize barely three per cent of its brain on the threshold of the twenty first century"

RANDOM THOUGHTS:

Close to 50 million Americans have no health care yet pay taxes that provide health care to illegal aliens.

Our government spends across the board over 30 billion annually on illegal aliens.

There are close to 400,000 homeless veterans in America.

There are on average, 80,000 chemicals in each American home. 90% of them are untested.

Over three (3) billion prescriptions are written each year.

The greatest challenge in the world is to successfully raise a child. The second greatest is to practice reproductive restraint.

No one has the right to smoke. We sue tobacco companies and then subsidize them so that they can afford the judgments.

Wall Street brokers are pecuniary pimps.

The fact that incest occurs at all is both an indictment and testimony to our primitive nature.

A title such as King and Queen, Prince and Princess, Lord and Lady are repulsive in both implication and application. Simply referring to a Hollywood celebrity as a star is repulsive. Stars exist in the sky.

There were 30 known exorcisms performed by the Catholic Church in 2000. Lucifer literally means "morning star"

The latest studies indicate that babies who are breast fed for at least a year have higher IQ's. It is not true that adult men trying to play "catch up" will be rewarded with higher IQ's.

180,000 African Americans fought in the Civil War. 33,000 of them died. In 1866 Congress created the first African American military units. They were the 9th and 10th Calvary and served with distinction known as the "Buffalo Soldiers"

Twenty four percent of all Gulf War deaths were from "friendly fire" The term "friendly fire" is an insult to those who died.

Over 60,000 Viet Nam Veterans have committed suicide. 58,000 others were killed in action.

Close to 8 million pets are killed in animal shelters annually.

Over 4,000 dogs served with the military in Viet Nam. 204 of them survived.

Humans and primates have the same number of hairs per square inch on their bodies.

In the final stages of development in the womb, the fetus is completely covered with hair. Approximately

ONE MONTH PRIOR TO BIRTH MOST OF THE HAIR FALLS OFF AND IS REMOVED WITH THE AFTERBIRTH. IN THE LATER YEARS OF A MAN'S LIFE THE HAIR REGENERATES IN AND ON THE EARS, NOSE, AND TESTICLES.

THERE ARE MORE THAN 30 MILLION SINGLE FAMILY HOMES IN AMERICA. 90% OF THEM ARE LED BY WOMEN.

MEN BATTER FIVE MILLION WOMEN A YEAR.

30,000 CHILDREN IN THE WORLD DIE EVERY DAY FROM NEGLECT AND STARVATION. CHINA STILL ABANDONS OR PUTS TO DEATH FEMALE INFANTS.

THE AFRICAN AMERICAN DOCTOR WHO DISCOVERED/INVENTED PLASMA WAS DENIED TREATMENT FOLLOWING AN AUTOMOBILE ACCIDENT IN THE SOUTH. THE DOCTOR DIED.

CHIEF GEORGE OF THE NEZ PERCE TRIBE LITERALLY DIED OF A BROKEN HEART.

THE AMERICAN GOVERNMENT BROKE MORE THAN 500 TREATY'S WITH NATIVE AMERICANS.

REGARDING THE CONDUCT OF THE UNITED STATES CONGRESS: 29 HAVE BEEN ACCUSED OF SPOUSAL ABUSE, 7 HAVE BEEN ARRESTED FOR FRAUD, 19 HAVE BEEN ACCUSED OF WRITING BAD CHECKS, 117 OF THEM HAVE DIRECTLY OR INDIRECTLY BANKRUPTED AT LEAST 2 BUSINESSES, 3 HAVE DONE TIME FOR ASSAULT, 71 CANNOT GET A CREDIT CARD BECAUSE OF BAD CREDIT, 14 HAVE BEEN ARRESTED ON DRUG RELATED CHARGES, 84 HAVE BEEN ARRESTED FOR DUI IN 2000, AND 8 HAVE BEEN ARRESTED FOR SHOPLIFTING.

APHIDS LIVE FOR THREE WEEKS. THEIR OFFSPRING ARE BORN PREGNANT THEREBY DOING AWAY WITH THE TEDIOUS AND ARDUOUS EFFORTS COMMON TO COURTSHIP.

THERE ARE AT LEAST 100 BILLION OTHER GALAXIES SIMILAR TO OURS. THERE ARE AT LEAST 400 BILLION SUNS SIMILAR TO OURS

IN THOSE GALAXIES. WE ARE THE CARTOONS THAT AMUSE AND ENTERTAIN THE INTELLIGENT BEINGS IN THOSE OTHER GALAXIES.

TABLE OF CONTENTS

RxAMERICA

A Script for Survival

Preface:

Planet Earth is rapidly becoming an orbiting outhouse, long on poop and short on toilet paper. That is not the spotted owl's fault. It is the result of a species of animal that globally bumps uglies without any thought or regard to consequence individually or collectively. Thus the planet's human population increases geometrically, feeding like locusts on all other living things until, as is happening now in some parts of the world, representatives of Homo Rectum turn inward and began feeding on themselves, thus conforming literally to the definition of a disease.

Humans are one of 50 billion species of life occupying earth in various stages of evolution. More than 50,000 species of animal and plant life are destroyed each year because of the human animal's intrusion into their habitats.

Most census takers and sociologists agree that the world population will be at or exceed 12 billion by the middle of the twenty first century. It took approximately 400,000 years to populate the earth with the first billion people. We arrived there in 1800. We added another 700,000 between 1800 and 1870. From the year 1870 to the present we have processed onto the planet, another five plus billion. The expansion of our species is the result of advances in the technologies influencing medicine, agriculture, distribution systems, safety, communication, and transportation. No thought or consideration was ever given to excesses; especially regarding family size or more appropriately, earth sustaining size.

ALL AGREE THAT LESS THAN 20% OF THE PEOPLE ON EARTH CONSUME MORE THAN 80% OF THE PLANET'S RESOURCES.

A CASE IN POINT; EVEN THE MOST DISPARATE OF GROUPS AGREE THAT CENTRAL AFRICA'S POPULATION WILL DOUBLE IN THE NEXT TWENTY FIVE YEARS. AS IS ALREADY HAPPENING, THE SHEER NUMBERS OF PEOPLE WILL OVERWHELM THE ENVIRONMENT, FORESTS WILL DISAPPEAR HAVING BEEN LOGGED FOR BUILDING AND CLEARED FOR GRAZING, AND ALL OTHER FORMS OF ANIMAL LIFE WILL BE EATEN. EVENTUALLY, WITH NO OTHER FOOD SOURCE IN THE BARREN AND ARID REGION, THE CONTINUALLY COUPLING PEOPLE WILL EXPERIENCE MASS DISEASE, STARVATION, AND RESORT IN THEIR FINAL DAYS, TO CANNIBALISM.

ONCE AGAIN THERE EXIST CERTAIN TRUTHS CONCERNING THE HUMAN CONDITION.

IN TERMS OF AN HISTORICAL COSMIC PERSPECTIVE, WE AS A SPECIES ARE BRAND NEW. ONLY RECENTLY DISCOVERED VIRUSES AND INFECTIONS CAN CLAIM TO BE THE LATEST INHABITANTS OF MOTHER EARTH, AND ONLY WHEN WE ACKNOWLEDGE THE COMPARISON CAN WE HOPE TO REVERSE COURSE AND AFFECT SOME KIND OF CHANGE.

HOMO SAPIEN IS AN ANIMAL, PURE AND SIMPLE. IT IS A BI-PEDAL SPECIES THAT USES LESS THAN THREE PER-CENT OF ITS BRAIN YET CLAIMS TO HAVE CONQUERED OR SOLVED MOST OF THE MYSTERIES OF THE UNIVERSE.

THE SPECIES HAS NO INHERENT DIVINE CONNECTION SAVE THE SELF MADE FABRICATIONS OF SELF-SERVING SOLICITORS. THAT IS NOT TO SAY THAT A DIVINE BEING DOES NOT EXIST, I BELIEVE ONE DOES, ALONG WITH A HOST OF ANGELS AND OTHER ANCILLARY ENTITIES. GRACE IS ACHIEVED THROUGH EVOLUTION AND SPIRITUAL GROWTH, NOT SIMPLY BY BEING BORN.

THE HUMAN ANIMAL IS NOT INTELLECTUALLY READY FOR NOR PREPARED TO UNDERSTAND THE TRUE NATURE OF ITS EXISTENCE; PERHAPS WHEN OUR SPECIES IS USING THE OTHER NINETY-EIGHT PER-CENT OF ITS SOFT WARE THAT MIGHT BE POSSIBLE.

OTHER THAN THE CHAPTER ON GOD, THERE WILL BE NO DISCUSSION OF RELIGION OR THEOLOGY IN THIS BOOK FOR ONCE AGAIN, THOSE CONSIDERATIONS SHOULD REMAIN ROOTED IN THE FERTILE FIELDS OF PERSONAL FAITH AND NOT IN PUBLIC PRONOUNCEMENTS BY ALLEGEDLY PERFECT PEOPLE HOPING TO CAPITALIZE ON A SPECIES COLLECTIVE FEAR AND CONFUSION OF THE UNKNOWN.

CREATIONISTS ARGUE THAT A COUPLE OF THOUSAND YEARS AGO THE GOOD LORD SNAPPED HIS FINGERS AND PRODUCED ADAM AND EVE ALONG WITH A SUPPORTIVE ECO-SYSTEM.

ARGUING ABOUT AND DWELLING ON DISCUSSIONS AND DEBATE ABOUT ORIGIN IS GOING TO DO NOTHING TO ASSIST WITH ADDRESSING THE CHALLENGES OF THE FUTURE.

WE AS A SPECIES ARE NOW OUT OF TIME.

SINCE WE EMERGED FROM THE CAVES PEOPLE HAVE DONE TWO THINGS WITH ABANDON, THEY'VE REPRODUCED, AND LAID CLAIM TO ALL THINGS AROUND THEM WHETHER IT BE LAND OR OTHER LIVING THINGS.

WE'VE REFERRED TO THESE EFFORTS AS PROGRESS.

WE'VE LAID WASTE TO THE WORLD IN THE NAME OF DEFENSE, DEITIES, AND DESTINY WHEN ALL IT REALLY EVER BOILED DOWN TO WAS GREED.

AS THE SUPERFICIAL, ALBEIT VISUAL, DIFFERENCES BECAME APPARENT TO THE OTHERWISE IDENTICAL SPECIES (SKIN COLOR, BODY TYPE, HABITS, AND CUSTOMS), A COLLECTIVE FEAR AND PARANOIA BECAME A PLAGUE AMONG AN EMERGING PEOPLE.

THE REAL CULPRIT IN ALL OF THIS IS MAN'S INNATE ANIMAL NATURE. WE BEHAVE EXACTLY AS DO OTHER FORMS OF ANIMAL LIFE. UNTIL, EITHER THROUGH DIVINE INTERVENTION OR COLLECTIVE INTROSPECTION, MAN ESCAPES HIS BONDS OF BRUTISHNESS, NOTHING WILL CHANGE. CALLING UP THE COURAGE TO CONTINUE BEYOND THE DIMLY LIT CUL DE SAC OF CONFUSION ON INTO THE LIGHT OF HOPE IS MAN'S ONLY CHANCE FOR SURVIVAL.

THE CLUBS WE USED AS CAVE DWELLERS FOR HUNTING AND DEFENSE HAVE BEEN REPLACED BY SMART BOMBS AND SATELLITES.

OUR DOMESTIC CLUBS HAVE METAPHORICALLY BECOME LETHAL PIECES OF LEGISLATION MOST OFTEN DESIGNED TO REPRESS AND HOLD HOSTAGE OTHER HUMANS AND LIVING THINGS THAT MIGHT JUST HAPPEN TO INHIBIT THE PROFIT OF A FEW.

THE NEW GOD OR ICON IS BUSINESS.

CHRISTIAN SOLDIERS HAVE BECOME CHRISTIAN BUSINESSMEN. THEIR PONTIFICATIONS AND PRAYERS ARE SELF-SERVING AND ISOLATIONIST. THEY HAVE TRULY BECOME THE GARGOYLES OF GREED.

IN THE 1990'S WE ARE PLAGUED WITH A PLETHORA OF PROBLEMS. MOST LIVING THINGS ARE BARELY AFLOAT ON A MAN MADE SEA OF SORROW WHILE DOZENS OF BLUE RIBBON COMMITTEES CONDUCT STUDIES NOT ABOUT WHERE IT ALL WENT WRONG, BUT HOW TO MAINTAIN THE STATUS QUO WHILE APPEASING THE MASSES.

TO REVERSE THE COURSE, TWO ACTIVITIES MUST OCCUR.

COLLECTIVELY AND INDIVIDUALLY, MAN MUST BECOME ACQUAINTED WITH HIS SPIRITUAL SELF. I DIDN'T SAY RELIGIOUS SELF, I SAID SPIRITUAL SELF. THAT CAN BE DONE EASILY THROUGH REFLECTION, INTROSPECTION, AND PRAYER AND HAS ABSOLUTELY NOTHING TO DO WITH EXISTING SECULAR INSTITUTIONS CLAIMING TO BE CONDUITS TO CHRIST. THE ANGELS ARE LISTENING.

BASED ON MAN'S FUNDAMENTAL ANIMAL NATURE, THE SOCIAL FABRIC OF OUR SOCIETY NEEDS TO BE RADICALLY ALTERED IN ORDER TO ATTEMPT TO ESTABLISH FAIRNESS, PARITY, AND EQUITY. THIS CAN ONLY BE ACCOMPLISHED BY ABSOLUTELY INSISTING THAT PEOPLE BE RESPONSIBLE FOR THEIR OWN BEHAVIOR AT EVERY LEVEL OF SOCIAL INVOLVEMENT.

While it remains true that we cannot change the world, I will offer solutions to most of America's social problems always with an eye on Mother Earth.

I have no illusions concerning the application of the remedies in the following chapters; I do know for sure that if radical changes are not made immediately in our social structure, revolution is inevitable, as it should be. Human conduct should be all about the oft stated and forgotten legal term "rights and corresponding duties" while always concerned about one another and the environment.

My approach is both pragmatic and compassionate and based in two truths, that one, man is nothing more than a high tech, atomic animal, and further that until he collectively and individually alters his behavior, society has a right to force him to behave responsibly.

The second truth is founded in my personal knowledge that life needn't be miserable for most, that while tears of sorrow are inevitable in a loving life, most should be shed joyously, that we all have Guardian Angels to guide us, and that it is up to us as individuals to make a conscious effort to not only attempt to live righteously, but to try to make as Harry Chapin said, the world "a better place to be".

MY VIEW

"LONG LINES, NEVER ENDING
FRUSTRATION BUILDING, BODIES BLENDING
A CHILD'S CRY, MOTHER TENDING
LONGER LINES, NEVER ENDING"

ALL THE FOLLOWING FIXES ARE FOUNDED IN MY BELIEF THAT WE AS A SPECIES ARE NOTHING MORE THAN DISPARATE SOULS ON PERSONAL JOURNEYS THROUGH A SERIES OF LIFETIMES WITHIN A SPECIFIC CONTEXT OF TIME, WITH THE GOAL ONCE AGAIN OF ACHIEVING SPIRITUAL GROWTH AND ULTIMATE PERFECTION.

AS AN EXAMPLE OF MY PHILOSOPHY/FEELINGS TO FOLLOW, I WILL TOUCH THE TOPICS OF REPRODUCTION AND ABORTION, TWO ISSUES THAT WILL BE ADDRESSED IN MORE DETAIL IN LATER CHAPTERS.

OUR BODIES ARE SIMPLY HOSTS OR VEHICLES FOR THE JOURNEY, REFERRED TO AS SUCH BECAUSE OF THE CERTAIN CHALLENGES AND TRAVAILS THAT ARE CERTAIN TO ACCOMPANY US EACH STEP OF THE WAY.

SOULS SEEKING A HOST IN WHICH TO INCARNATE ARE INNOCENT AND LACK ANY AGENDA. THEY ARE COMPLETELY DEPENDENT UPON THE CONDITION AND BEHAVIOR OF HOSTS, WHO FOR ALL PRACTICAL PURPOSES WILL BE THEIR NEW GUIDES OR PARENTS DURING THIS PERIOD IN THEIR EVOLUTION.

WE ALL GO THROUGH IT, AND WE ARE CURRENTLY INVOLVED IN THE PROCESS. THAT IS WHY IT IS SO IMPORTANT TO OFFER AN INCARNATING SOUL IN INFANT FORM THE BEST POSSIBLE BEGINNING FOR ITS NEW LIFE.

WHILE THE SOUL, THE ENERGY, THE SPARK OF LIGHT IS ETERNALLY SACRED, THE PHYSICAL HOST (THE BODY) IS NOT. IT REMAINS MERELY A VEHICLE DESIGNED TO CARRY THE SPIRIT DURING GESTATION.

IF FOR A VARIETY OF REASONS THE HOST(S) ARE ILL SUITED FOR THE TASK OF PARENTING, TERMINATION OR ABORTION IS NOT ONLY A REASONABLE OPTION BUT OFTEN DESIRABLE.

THE SOUL WILL VACATE THE BODY, RE-ENTER THE ETHERS, AND EVENTUALLY LOCATE A MORE SUITABLE OR HEALTHY HOST. IT'S AS SIMPLE AS THAT.

WE OWE IT TO OURSELVES AS AN EXTENDED AND STRUGGLING FAMILY TO OFFER THE BEST IN COMFORT, SAFETY, AND ACCOMMODATION TO THOSE SOULS WISHING TO CONTINUE THEIR QUEST DURING OUR SHIFT HERE ON EARTH.

PRACTITIONERS OF THE CHRISTIAN RIGHT A.K.A. RELIGIOUS WRONG WOULD HAVE US BELIEVE THAT ABORTION IS NOT ONLY A SIN BUT A CRIME. I SAY IT IS A CRIME TO INTRODUCE A CHILD (RE-INCARNATED SOUL) INTO AN ENVIRONMENT IN WHICH IT IS EITHER NOT WANTED (RAPE, INCEST, ACCIDENTAL OR UNPLANNED PREGNANCY), SUBJECTED TO PHYSICAL DEFORMITY AS A CONSEQUENCE OF IRRESPONSIBLE AND SELFISH BEHAVIOR (INGESTION OF DRUGS, ALCOHOL, OR NICOTINE), OR LACKS ANY CHANCE OR OPPORTUNITY FOR A HEALTHY, LOVING LIFE (TRAGIC EXAMPLES OF SUCH HABITATS EXIST ON EVERY CONTINENT THROUGHOUT THE WORLD), IN WHICH FOR ALL INTENTS AND PURPOSES THE NEW-BORN IS ABANDONED AT BIRTH AND LEFT TO FEND FOR ITSELF.

IT IS NOT RIGHT FOLKS; IT IS IMMORAL, UNENLIGHTENED, AND PRIMITIVE CONDUCT.

PERHAPS THE GOOD LORD HAD EVERYTHING TO DO WITH THE CREATION OF LIFE, BUT WITH THE EXCEPTION OF MIRACLES OR DIVINE INTERVENTION, HAS NOTHING TO DO WITH ITS DISPOSITION. IF MEN ARE THE MASTERS AS DICTATED BY THE BIBLE, THEY NEED TO BE HELD TO THE HIGHEST OF STANDARDS IN TERMS OF THEIR SOCIAL CONDUCT ALBEIT, BIRTH CONTROL, FAMILIAL SUPPORT, EDUCATION, ETC.

IT IS MY OPINION THAT HAVING A CHILD IS THE EPITOME OF SELFISHNESS AND ARROGANCE, AND ILLUSTRATES OUR UNENLIGHTENED NATURE AND IGNORANCE. I COULD NEVER BRING A CHILD/PERSON INTO THIS WORLD KNOWING THAT HE OR SHE

FACES A CERTAIN DEATH AND THE PROBABILITY OF PHYSICAL AND EMOTIONAL SUFFERING DURING THEIR LIFETIME.

HARSH AS IT MAY SOUND, IT MUST BE SAID; A CHILD THAT IS NOT GOING TO BE BORN INTO A HEALTHY, LOVING, NURTURING, AND COMPLETELY SUPPORTIVE ENVIRONMENT CAN OFTEN BE CONDEMNED TO A LIFE OF UNNECESSARY HARDSHIP AND DEPRIVATION WHEN THE REAL TRUTH IS THAT THE YOUNG ONE'S AGONY COULD HAVE AND SHOULD HAVE BEEN PREVENTED.

THE LIGHT/SOUL CAN BOUNCE BACK OUT, REGROUP AND RE-ENTER THROUGH ANOTHER PARENT BETTER EQUIPPED FOR THE CHALLENGE OF CHILDREN.

I CAN HEAR THEM NOW, THOSE SINGULARLY DIMENSIONAL DICTATORS OF DECENCY OFFERING EXAMPLES OF THOSE WHO OVERCAME AND "ROSE" TO THE OCCASION. IF THEY HAD ANY SENSE THEY'D BE EMBARRASSED FOR WHY, AFTER IT'S ALL BEEN ARGUED, WOULD ANYONE POSSESSING COMPASSION AND GRACE WISH THE WORST FOR ANY LIVING THING?

REPRODUCTION REMAINS THE NUMBER ONE PROBLEM IN THE WORLD.

UNTIL THE HUMAN ANIMAL CEASES TO IRRESPONSIBLY COUPLE WITHOUT REGARD TO CONSEQUENCE, SOCIETY HAS NOT ONLY A RIGHT BUT AN OBLIGATION TO FORCE RESPONSIBLE BEHAVIOR. SOME OF THOSE ISSUES WILL BE ADDRESSED IN FOLLOWING CHAPTERS.

ABORTION/TERMINATION IS TRAGIC. IT CERTAINLY CONFLICTS WITH THE NATURAL IMPULSES AND INSTINCTS OF THE HUMAN EXPERIENCE BUT IS NOT CONTRARY TO THE NATURAL ORDER OF LIFE.

ONE MUST DIFFERENTIATE BETWEEN DNA'S DESIRE FOR LIFE AND THE SELFISHNESS INHERENT IN IMPOSING AN UNFAIR, CRUEL, AND BURDENSOME LIFE ON A SOUL.

WOMEN SHOULD BE THE SOLE ARBITERS AND DECISION MAKERS CONCERNING THE ISSUE OF ABORTION. IT IS NOT THE PROVINCE OF

MEN. LEGISLATION REGARDING THE TOPIC SHOULD BE DEBATED ON AND VOTED ON BY WOMEN. THEY ARE ULTIMATELY THE PERSONS WHO WILL SUFFER THE GESTATION, BIRTH, AND UNFORTUNATELY IN INCREASING NUMBERS, BE THE SOLE PARENT OR PROVIDER.

I AM GOING TO INTRODUCE A NUMBER OF TOPICS (SOCIAL PROBLEMS) THAT I THINK NEED TO BE IDENTIFIED AND FIXED, FOLLOWED BY A BRIEF EXPLANATION OF THE PRESCRIPTION.

THE MONEY NECESSARY TO FUND THESE FIXES OR CHANGES WILL BE GENERATED BY COMPLETELY OVERHAULING THE IRS AND TAX SYSTEM (INCLUDING TAXING CHURCHES AND CLOSING VIRTUALLY ALL CORPORATE LOOPHOLES), BY SEIZURE OF ASSETS AS PUNISHMENT, BY ELIMINATING INEFFECTIVE DOMESTIC AND FOREIGN POLICIES, BY REDUCING THE NUMBERS OF MAJOR MILITARY WEAPONS PURCHASED, AND BY REGULATING BANKS ALONG WITH OTHER FINANCIAL INSTITUTIONS.

I AM GOING TO AVOID GETTING INTO SOME POLYSYLLABIC DISCOURSE ABOUT THE LIVING CONDITION. PHILOSOPHICAL IMPOSTORS WITH PENCHANTS FOR LITERARY PUFFING CAN CONTINUE TO AMUSE EACH OTHER DOING THAT IN THEIR STERILE CLIQUES.

MY TAKE ON THE PROBLEMS IS BASED ON MY KNOWLEDGE THAT UNTIL HUMAN NATURE METAMORPHOSIS'S FROM ITS PRIMITIVE STATE INTO A CONDITION OF PERPETUAL GRACE AND WISDOM, SOCIETY HAS THE ULTIMATE OBLIGATION TO FORCE THE ANIMAL WE CALL HUMAN TO BEHAVE RESPONSIBLY.

Abortion, Birth Control, and Child Care

"What are children after all, but extensions
of ego seasoned with subliminal implications of
immortality?"

Abortion:

As indicated in My View, the sole arbiters or decision makers concerning the subject of abortion should be women. However, the woman in me feels strongly about the following.

An abortion should be available to anyone at no cost up to the fifth month of pregnancy.

No abortions should be performed after the fifth month unless the mother's life is in danger, or if there is irrefutable evidence that the new born will be either physically or mentally unable to function as an autonomous living being.

If testing proves conclusively that the defects or disabilities are the direct result of irresponsible behavior on the mother's part, she will be sterilized. If any man whether it be the biological father, boyfriend, step-father, or criminal, causes injury to a pregnant woman in such a way as to injure or kill her fetus, he/she will be sterilized and locked up for life without parole.

All pre-natal care, all therapy, and all surgical procedures relative to an abortion will be free to all citizens of the United States.

Consistent with opinions expressed in following chapters under Health Care and Welfare, no pregnant women will be denied housing, clothing, nutrition, or access to any clinic or hospital.

5

ANY INDIVIDUAL OR GROUP THAT ATTEMPTS TO PREVENT ACCESS TO THE ABOVE WILL BE CHARGED WITH A FELONY, AND IF CONVICTED, WILL HAVE THOSE ASSETS SEIZED TO THE EXTENT THE SPECIFIC ASSETS WERE USED IN COMMISSION OF THE OFFENCE. IF A CAR(S) WAS USED AS TRANSPORTATION TO THE SITE OF THE PROTEST, IT OR THEY WILL BE SEIZED. THE BUILDING(S) USED IN THE PLANNING, OR PREPARATION (SIGNS, BANNERS, ETC.) WILL BE SEIZED REGARDLESS WHETHER OR NOT IT IS A CHURCH. THE PARTICIPANTS WILL BE FINED THE EQUIVALENT OF ONE YEAR'S WAGES AT THEIR CURRENT OR PAST JOB AND THE FUNDS WILL BE RECOVERED AS URGENTLY AS IF THE MONEY WAS STOLEN FROM THE POPE'S OWN POCKET.

IT IS MY OPINION THAT THE COWARDLY AND UNENLIGHTENED RELIGIOUS WRONG WILL ONLY INVOLVE THEMSELVES IN A CIVIL PROTEST IF IT IS CONVENIENT AND AFFORDABLE. THE FIRST AMENDMENT DOES NOT PROVIDE THE RIGHT FOR ONE PERSON TO DENY ANOTHER THEIRS. WHEN THE DIALOGUE AMONG THOSE WHO DISAGREE BECOMES PHYSICAL, CONSTITUTIONAL PROTECTION NO LONGER APPLIES.

BIRTH CONTROL:

ONCE AGAIN, THE TWO PRIMARY CAUSES OF THE CHAOS AND CRUELTY IN THE WORLD CAN DIRECTLY BE ATTRIBUTED TO OVERPOPULATION AND ITS COHORT, A PRIMITIVE AND LIMITED COLLECTIVE INTELLECT EXISTING IN HUMAN/ANIMAL NATURE.

ONE OF COURSE LEADS TO THE OTHER. IF WE AS A SPECIES WEREN'T SO UNENLIGHTENED AND ARROGANT, BIRTH CONTROL WOULDN'T BE A PROBLEM. WE WOULD HAVE UNDERSTOOD THE RAMIFICATIONS OF RAMPANT REPRODUCTION AND BEHAVED ACCORDINGLY. THAT IS OBVIOUSLY NOT THE CASE; CONSEQUENTLY WE ARE FORCED TO REACT TO OUR FAILED FORESIGHT WITH SOMETIMES HARSH AND RADICAL PRESCRIPTIONS.

NO COUPLE IN AMERICA, FROM THE PRESENT ON, SHOULD BE ALLOWED TO HAVE MORE THAN TWO CHILDREN REGARDLESS OF RACE, WEALTH, OR POSITION. NO COUPLE IMMIGRATING INTO THE

United States would be allowed to bring more than two children.

What are children after all, but extensions of ego seasoned with subliminal implications of immortality?

The more disturbing and understandably unpalatable truth is that by bringing life into the world, parents are sentencing their children to death. In the galactic scheme of things, such sacrifice may be necessary to preserve the species; however, such cruel acts should be limited to two per family.

The initial justification for large families concerned the need for security especially in territorial disputes. Following the industrial revolution and the subsequent consolidations of family farms and businesses into giant conglomerates, the need for available and cheap family labor ceased to exist.

Apart from that, who has the right to bring another living being into this world only to be imprisoned in a forced agenda, or to become essentially indentured servants to the pedestrian aspirations of the parents. Ideally each generation should become more aware, better educated, and more inclined to question the status quo, and in so doing, learn, and with that knowledge grow personally and spiritually.

Anyone male or female who has already sired two children either separately or together, then bring a third into the world, will be permanently sterilized. No excuses! I can hear it now, the protestations from the fool who had several kids with his first wife, is now divorced, and the new wife (who hadn't had any children) wants one with him. Tough! Try it and you will be the proud owner of a pair of dysfunctional vas deferens.

The rule applies indiscriminately to everyone, from the wealthiest to the poor. Violators will not only be sterilized, they will be forced to pay for the procedure.

DAVID HAYDEN

IT IS NOT MANDATED ANYWHERE THAT A PERSON HAS TO HAVE A BABY. FOR THOSE WHO ARE UNABLE, OR THOSE WHO WOULD LIKE MORE THAN TWO CHILDREN, <u>ADOPT.</u> BUT SEE, THAT GETS BACK INTO THE PRIMAL EGO THING, "I WANT IT TO BE A PART OF ME" SYNDROME WHICH IS DISGUSTING IN ITS SUPERFICIALITY.

THE ONLY EXCEPTIONS TO THE TWO CHILD RULE WOULD BE WHERE A COUPLE HAD TWO, AND ONE OR BOTH DIED TRAGICALLY AS A RESULT OF ACCIDENT OR ILLNESS. THEY SHOULD BE ALLOWED TO HAVE ANOTHER IF THEY SO DESIRE. OR, IF A MAN LOST HIS PREGNANT WIFE AND UNBORN CHILD IN AN ACCIDENT, HE OF COURSE SHOULD BE ABLE TO TRY AGAIN WITH A WOMAN WHO HASN'T ALREADY HAD TWO.

ALL BIRTH CONTROL DEVICES (PILLS, PATCHES, IMPLANTS, CONDOMS, ETC.) AND SURGERIES (TUBULE LEGATIONS AND VASECTOMIES) SHOULD BE FREE AND READILY AVAILABLE TO ALL THE PUBLIC.

ANY PERSON WHO INTERFERES WITH ANY ASPECT OF BIRTH CONTROL PROMOTION WILL BE FINED AND/OR INCARCERATED DEPENDING OF COURSE, ON THE CIRCUMSTANCES SURROUNDING HIS/HER INVOLVEMENT.

CLONING OF ANY KIND IS A FELONY. LABORATORIES WILL BE SEIZED, SOLD, AND/OR DESTROYED. UPPER LEVEL MANAGEMENT WILL HAVE THEIR PERSONAL ASSETS SEIZED. WE AS A SPECIES ARE NOT AT THE STAGE OF OUR EVOLUTION WHERE WE SHOULD EVEN CONSIDER CLONING. THOUSANDS OF YEARS FROM NOW, IF WE ARE STILL AROUND, IT MIGHT POSSIBLY BE A SUBJECT FOR DISCUSSION ALTHOUGH ONLY AS AN EXISTENTIAL EXERCISE; BY THAT TIME OUR ABILITY TO REASON SHOULD RELEGATE CLONING KINDS OF CONSIDERATIONS TO SILLY DISCUSSIONS OF HOW IT WAS "WAY BACK THEN IN THE 1900'S".

CHILD CARE:

AS STATED BEFORE IN THE PREFACE, REINCARNATING SOULS DESERVE THE BEST SOCIETY (IN THE ROLE OF EXTENDED PARENTS) HAS TO OFFER.

EVERY CHILD SHOULD HAVE ACCESS TO THE BEST IN HEALTH CARE.

EVERY CHILD HAS THE RIGHT TO BE SAFE FROM HARM WHETHER THAT BE IN THE FORM OF NEGLECT, EXTERNAL INFLUENCE, AND PHYSICAL OR EMOTIONAL ABUSE.

EVERY CHILD SHOULD BE PROPERLY CLOTHED, HOUSED, FED, EDUCATED, AND NURTURED (LOVED, CUDDLED, PAMPERED, AND APPROPRIATELY DISCIPLINED).

ANY PARENT THAT FAILS TO PROVIDE ANY OF THE ABOVE (PARTICULARLY SINCE IN OUR WORLD THE GOODS AND SERVICES ARE FREE AND ACCESSIBLE) WILL FORFEIT THE PRIVILEGE. THE CHILD WILL BE PLACED IN EITHER A PUBLIC OR PRIVATE HABITAT THAT IS BETTER SUITED TO THE CHALLENGES OF CHILD CARE. THE PARENT(S) WILL BE EVALUATED FOR ABILITY AND HELPED IF AT ALL POSSIBLE TO REACH A LEVEL OF COMPETENCE THAT WOULD ALLOW A "MOTHER AND CHILD REUNION" TO OCCUR.

IF THE PARENT(S) ARE CLEARLY UNFIT, ANY FUNDS THEY HAVE AVAILABLE WILL BE USED TOWARD THE WELFARE OF THEIR CHILD, AND THEY WILL BE TEMPORARILY STERILIZED. IF EITHER ONE OF THE PARENTS HAS ALREADY HAD TWO KIDS THEY WILL BE PERMANENTLY STERILIZED.

ANY PRIVATE BUSINESS WITH OVER FIFTEEN EMPLOYEES AND ALL GOVERNMENTAL AGENCIES SHOULD BE REQUIRED TO PROVIDE DAY CARE. THIS INCLUDES LARGE COMPANIES WITH MOST OF ITS LABOR FORCE SITUATED IN SMALL SATELLITE OFFICES. FAILURE TO DO SO WOULD RESULT IN FINES EXCEEDING THE COST OF WHAT THE DAY CARE WOULD HAVE COST ORIGINALLY PLUS ONE YEAR'S ANNUAL PROFIT.

CHILDREN ARE OUR FUTURE. EMPHASIS NEEDS TO MOVE FROM SELF TO THE COMMON GOOD. IF ONE TRULY CARES ABOUT THE QUALITY OF LIFE FOR ALL LIVING THINGS, THAN LESS IS MORE (NUMBERS OF KIDS PER FAMILY), THEREFORE ALLOWING MORE CHILDREN ACROSS THE SPECTRUM OF SOCIETY ACCESS TO THE TOOLS NECESSARY TO COMPETENTLY AND CONFIDENTLY ASSUME

TOMORROW'S REINS. ALL BEINGS BENEFIT, NOT JUST A FORTUNATE FEW.

CRIME AND PUNISHMENT

"THERE IS AN ANALOGY BETWEEN THE EFFECT INSIDE TRADERS AND JUNK BONDERS CONDUCT HAS ON JOHN Q. CITIZEN AND THE B-52 PILOT WHO RELEASES HIS EXPLOSIVE CARGO 50,000 FEET ABOVE HIS VICTIMS"

CRIME HAS EXISTED AT SOME LEVEL SINCE PEOPLE BEGAN POPULATING THE PLANET. IN THE TWENTIETH CENTURY, CONTRARY CULTURES REACT DIFFERENTLY TO CRIMINAL BEHAVIOR.

A THIEF'S HAND WILL BE CUT OFF IN INDIA, WHEREAS THE UNITED STATES WILL SENTENCE A THIEF TO A LITTLE JAIL TIME WITH POSSIBLY A SMALL FINE. THE FINE IS HARDLY EVER PAID AND THE JAIL TIME IS REDUCED OR WAIVED BECAUSE OF OVERCROWDING AND A JUDICIAL SYSTEM ON THE VERGE OF COLLAPSE FROM THE WEIGHT OF ITS CASELOAD.

THERE'S NOT A LOT OF THEFT IN INDIA. THEFT IS RAMPANT IN THE UNITED STATES.

CUTTING OFF SOMEONE'S HAND IS NOT THE ANSWER, LETTING THEM GO ISN'T EITHER.

AT SOME POINT RATIONAL DECISIONS NEED TO BE MADE REGARDING SOCIAL CONDUCT BASED ON THE FUNDAMENTAL NATURE OF THE HUMAN ANIMAL.

IF A MEMBER OF SOCIETY BEHAVES IN A DISRUPTIVE OR UNACCEPTABLE WAY, HE/SHE NEEDS TO HUMANELY YET EXPEDITIOUSLY BE REBUKED AND/OR REMOVED FROM THE PUBLIC AT LARGE.

MOST PEOPLE KNOW, PARTICULARLY PEOPLE OF COLOR, POOR PEOPLE, AND PHYSICALLY CHALLENGED PEOPLE, THAT JUSTICE HAS A PRICE TAG TOO HIGH FOR MOST FOLKS TO AFFORD.

JUSTICE FOR ALL IS AN ILLUSION.

CONVERSELY, SIMPLY BECAUSE A PERSON IS BORN INTO UNFORTUNATE CIRCUMSTANCES, MAY BE IMPOVERISHED, MIGHT HAVE BEEN ABUSED, MAY HAVE BEEN OR BE THE OBJECT OF DISCRIMINATION, OR SUFFERED GOD KNOWS WHAT AT THE HANDS OF FATE OR FOOLS, DOES NOT GIVE THAT INDIVIDUAL THE RIGHT TO VIOLENTLY INVADE THE SPACE OF ANOTHER LIVING THING AS A REMEDY FOR THEIR DISTRESS OR MEANS OF SURVIVAL.

THIS IS THE UNFORTUNATE CONSEQUENCE OF A SPECIES REPRODUCING GEOMETRICALLY WHILE LIVING IN AN ARITHMETIC ENVIRONMENT. WE ARE ANIMALS WITH SPIRITUAL POTENTIAL; BUT REMAIN ANIMALS NONETHELESS.

DARWIN'S LAW IS WORKING IN THE SENSE THAT THOSE WHO HAVE HISTORICALLY BEEN PREYED UPON ARE NOW BECOMING PREDATORS.

IN SUBSEQUENT CHAPTERS I WILL DISCUSS HEALTH CARE, HOUSING, FOOD, EDUCATION, INFRASTRUCTURE, ETC., AND MOST IMPORTANTLY HOPE; ALL AMENITIES THAT SHOULD BE AVAILABLE TO EACH AND EVERY MEMBER OF A CIVILIZED SOCIETY.

HOWEVER, WE AS A PEOPLE CANNOT ALLOW CRIMINAL BEHAVIOR TO CONTINUE TO CHIP AWAY AT THE IDEAL OR THE DREAM, OR TO ALLOW VIOLENT AND/OR ANTI-SOCIAL BEHAVIOR TO SHAPE THE STRUCTURE OF OUR COUNTRY.

IT IS MY FEELING THAT ALL CRIME IS VIOLENT TO ONE DEGREE OR ANOTHER. CERTAINLY (TO USE THE OFT QUOTED EXAMPLE), A PERSON STEALING A LOAF OF BREAD TO FEED HIMSELF OR FAMILY IS ENTIRELY DIFFERENT THAN A DAHMER WHO KILLED PEOPLE AND THEN ATE THEM. DAHMER'S CRIME IS OBVIOUS IN ITS HORROR. BUT THE STUFF THAT HAPPENED TO THE PERSON THAT STOLE THE LOAF OF BREAD, THE EXCLUSION FROM OPPORTUNITY, OR DENIAL OF ASSISTANCE WITH A DISABILITY, OR SIMPLY A SOCIETIES REFUSAL TO ACKNOWLEDGE AND HELP SOMEONE WHO'S FALLEN ON HARD TIMES THROUGH NO REAL FAULT OF THEIR OWN, IS ANOTHER FORM OF VIOLENCE, A KIND THAT BURROWS INTO ONE'S PSYCHE PERMANENTLY AFFECTING ONE'S EMOTIONS BECAUSE, AFTER ALL, IT SHOULDN'T BE THAT WAY IN A COMPASSIONATE AND KIND COMMUNITY.

I'LL BEGIN WITH WHITE COLLAR CRIME WHICH I BELIEVE TO BE EVERY BIT AS VIOLENT AND IN SOME INSTANCES MORE AGONIZING IN IT'S RAMIFICATIONS AND LONG TERM EFFECT ON LARGE NUMBERS OF UNSUSPECTING AND DISASSOCIATED PEOPLE, THAN THAT PERPETRATED BY GOONS WITH GUNS AND KNIVES. AT LEAST THOSE VICTIMS HAVE VERY LITTLE TIME TO CONSIDER THEIR SITUATION OR MORTALITY.

WHITE COLLAR CRIME:

I'M NOT TALKING ABOUT THE COMMON CITIZEN WHO CHEATS ON HIS/HER TAXES HERE, I'M REFERRING TO THE CORPORATE CRIMINALS WHO HAVE ACCESS TO AND MANIPULATE THE MONEY IN AMERICA TO THE DETRIMENT OF THEIR INVESTORS AND/OR EMPLOYEES.

THE TWO MOST MENTIONED WORDS IN CORPORATE AMERICA IN THE 1990'S ARE MERGER AND DOWNSIZING.

MERGING IS A SUBJECT THAT COULD FILL A SEPARATE BOOK, WHAT CONCERNS ME IS THE <u>EFFECT</u> THE ACTION HAS ON THE EMPLOYEES OF THE TWO OR MORE COMBINING COMPANIES.

A SERIES OF FEDERAL GUIDELINES AND LAWS SHOULD BE PASSED REGARDING THE WELFARE OF THE FOLKS WHO LABORED LONG AND HARD FOR MANAGEMENT IN THEIR RESPECTIVE COMPANIES AND FIND THEMSELVES BEING TREATED AS PROPERTY ONCE THE UNION HAD OCCURRED.

FIRST, NO EMPLOYEE SHOULD LOSE THEIR JOB AS A RESULT OF THE MERGER. ANY EMPLOYEE REDUCTION SHOULD BE ACCOMPLISHED THROUGH ATTRITION (RETIREMENT, RESIGNATION), EARLY BUYOUTS (ONLY IF EMPLOYEE AGREES TO IT), OR UNFORTUNATE AND UNANTICIPATED PERSONAL DISASTER (DEATH, DISEASE, OR INJURY).

SECOND, NO PROFIT TAKING OF ANY KIND WILL BE ALLOWED WITHIN THE NEWLY COMBINED COMPANIES AT ANY LEVEL OF MANAGEMENT FOR FIVE YEARS. NO ACQUISITION OR CASHING IN OF STOCK, NO BONUSES OTHER THAN THE NORMAL CHRISTMAS

OR ANNUAL GIFT (AFTER MERGER NOT TO EXCEED THE DOLLAR AMOUNT OF THE MOST GENEROUS GIFT THE YEAR BEFORE), NO INCREASES IN CORPORATE SALARIES BEYOND THAT OF COST OF LIVING (SINGLE DIGIT PERCENTILE), AND NO PERKS OR GIFTS THAT COULD SERVE TO CIRCUMVENT THE INTENT OF THE RESTRICTIONS.

THIRD, THE NEW AND LARGER COMPANY WOULD BE REQUIRED TO OFFER COMPLETE HEALTH CARE, 401K, AND LIFE INSURANCE TO ALL ITS EMPLOYEES. THEY WOULD ALSO BE REQUIRED TO STRICTLY ADHERE TO GOVERNMENT GUIDELINES CONCERNING "GLASS CEILINGS" FOR WOMEN AND PEOPLE OTHER THAN MALE CAUCASIANS.

FOURTH, THE NEW COMPANY SHOULD RECEIVE NO INCENTIVES OR TAX BREAKS REGARDING THEIR EFFORTS TO UNITE. THAT WOULD BE THE FINANCIAL EQUIVALENT OF A STRANGER OFFERING A COUPLE HELP WITH COITUS WHEN THEY WERE OBVIOUSLY CAPABLE OF ACCOMPLISHING THE TASK BY THEMSELVES.

THE MOST DISTURBING OF ALL WHITE COLLAR CRIME IS THAT IT IS PERPETRATED ON THE TENS OF THOUSANDS OF UNSUSPECTING AND WELL INTENTIONED PEOPLE BY THE SAVINGS AND LOAN BARONS AND THE JUNK BOND BURGLARS OR ANY OF THE MONEY MANAGERS WHO PARLAYED ILLEGAL FINANCIAL TRANSACTIONS INTO PERSONAL FORTUNES.

THE PROBLEM HAS ALWAYS BEEN THAT BIG MONEY AND THE LEGAL SYSTEM ARE ALLIES. IT'S ALL ABOUT THE TRANSFER OF DOLLARS TO ONE ANOTHER OR KEEPING IT IN THE CIRCLE. MILKEN, BOSKY, AND KEATING, TO NAME BUT A FEW, RIP OFF A COUPLE HUNDRED THOUSAND PEOPLE, GET BUSTED, PAY THEIR HIGH PRICED ATTORNEYS WITH THEIR VICTIMS MONEY, PAY A FINE THAT CONSTITUTES A FRACTION OF THE TOTAL TAKE (SOME OF WHICH TRICKLES BACK TO THE VICTIMS; THANK YOU RONNIE FOR THE DEFICIT), SPEND A LITTLE TIME IN A COUNTRY CLUB, AND GET TO KEEP THEIR MANSIONS, MAINTAIN THEIR LUXURIOUS LIFESTYLE, AND <u>KEEP</u> MOST OF THE STOLEN MONEY. THAT IS DISGUSTING!

THE SOLUTION IS SIMPLE, UNFORTUNATELY THE ENFORCEMENT IS NOT.

Using the Maggot Milken as an example, he should have been incarcerated for life in a Federal Penitentiary. All of his money and assets should have been recovered and used to fully repay his victims. Any left should have been used to pay for his prosecution and confinement. All that he should own in terms of personal property is a toothbrush and a Bible; he doesn't need a comb. Everything else should be confiscated and considered the property of the people of the United States of America.

The same sentence should apply to all the CEO's, Presidents, and Managers who piloted the failed savings and loans, sold junk bonds, or committed insurance or any other kind of fraud.

How anyone can pretend parity or fairness exists, when a maggot like Milken does a few years, keeps 500 million, and becomes a celebrity, compared to the small business owner who cheats on his taxes (in an inherently unfair system), loses virtually everything, and is marked for life. The small guy gets the slammer, and goes bankrupt while the big time burglars do talk shows, lecture, and sell books.

Pursuing and properly punishing the practitioners of white collar crime would provide much of the money necessary to mend the social fabric their behavior ripped apart.

If you consider Milken and his fellow maggots non-violent criminals, try to convince the family whose father committed suicide after he saw his life turn to shit following his association with alleged legitimate investment companies that were in fact funny money factories or junk bond bordellos.

There is an analogy between the effect inside traders and junk bonders conduct has on John Q. Citizen and the B-52 pilot who releases his explosive cargo 50,000 feet above his victims.

Another group of individuals that deserve the harshest of punishment are those who prey on Senior citizens, the physically challenged, or the mentally impaired. These creeps use insurance fraud, contracting schemes, and mortgage manipulation to coerce the vulnerable through threat, intimidation, and fear (most often associated with death and dying) into parting with what little money they have left in the twilight of their lives. When convicted, these scum should be relieved of all of their personal assets, and be forced to spend the remainder of their time on Earth performing mandatory community service.

Street Crime:

Since the time when the population of the world exceeded one, some kind of domination has occurred. One spouse dominated the other, a behavior learned and continued by their children, the stronger neighbor dominated the weaker, with the corollary extending on to towns, counties, states, and nations ad infinitum, and while pursuing that basic instinct to control, reaffirming man's animal nature. When the domination becomes criminal, it's got to be stopped, and the causes of the criminal behavior, as much as can be ascertained, have to be removed.

Soft Crime:

Penalties for "soft" crimes such as shoplifting cosmetics, stealing groceries, and siphoning gas, need to be more responsive to the problem rather than be punitive in nature.

Reasons for doing any of the above run the gamut from poor self esteem, to hunger, to maybe even a desperate need to get somewhere. Or the perps could simply be irresponsible assholes. For the first offence, they should be given the benefit of the doubt.

Therapy might be appropriate for the cosmetic caper. If the person really needs food, then get the individual some food stamps and provide access to long term help so

THAT HE/SHE CAN IMPROVE THEIR LIFE SITUATION. AT MINIMUM, THE PERSON SIPHONING GAS SHOULD REPAY THE COST OF WHAT WAS TAKEN ALONG WITH ANY DAMAGE, AND SHOULD PROBABLY GO WASH PUBLIC WORKS VEHICLES FOR A WEEKEND.

IF THE PERPS ARE JUVENILES, THEIR PARENTS SHOULD BE HELD COMPLETELY LIABLE. IF THE PARENTS ARE UNFIT, THE CHILD SHOULD BE REMANDED TO A FOSTER HOME OR YOUTH FACILITY WITH THE COST TO BE BORN BY THE PARENTS. IF EITHER THE FATHER OR MOTHER HAS ALREADY PRODUCED TWO CHILDREN, THEY WILL BE REMINDED THAT TWO'S THE LIMIT. IF THEY ARE ACTIVELY ENGAGING IN CRIMINAL BEHAVIOR, THEY WILL BE PROSECUTED AND STERILIZED.

PENALTIES FOR SECOND OFFENCES OF "SOFT" CRIMES SHOULD AVOID INCARCERATION IF POSSIBLE. CONFISCATE SOMETHING THAT IS OF VALUE TO THE PERSON; A BOOM BOX OR TV. SUPPLEMENT THAT WITH MANDATORY COUNSELING AND/OR THERAPY ALONG WITH COMMUNITY SERVICE (REMOVING GRAFFITI, WASHING SCHOOL BUSES, SWEEPING SIDEWALKS ON CITY STREETS).

THIRD OFFENCE AND THEY ARE OFF THE STREET.

MUCH OF THE ADJUDICATION FOR A MISDEMEANOR VIOLATION SHOULD BE DONE IN A FAMILY OR COMMUNITY COURT SETTING THEREBY LIGHTENING TO SOME EXTENT THE CASELOAD OF MUNICIPAL, STATE, AND FEDERAL COURTS SO THAT THEY MAY DEAL WITH THE MORE SERIOUS CRIMES.

HARD CRIME:

OVERTLY VIOLENT CRIME IS UNACCEPTABLE UNDER ANY CIRCUMSTANCE. NO ONE HAS THE RIGHT TO VIOLENTLY INVADE ANOTHER PERSON'S SPACE OR LIFE. IF THEY DO SO THEY SHOULD BE AT RISK.

THE POLICE CAN NO LONGER BE EXPECTED TO PROVIDE A SAFE AND SECURE ENVIRONMENT FOR EVERY CITIZEN TWENTY-FOUR HOURS A DAY. INCREASINGLY IT IS INCUMBENT UPON ALL ADULT INDIVIDUALS TO ASSUME RESPONSIBILITY FOR BOTH THEM AND THEIR FAMILY'S SAFETY. PEOPLE NEED TO BE TAUGHT HOW

TO CONTROL THEIR SURROUNDINGS IN TERMS OF SAFETY RATHER THAN BEING COMPROMISED BY AN ENCLOSED SITUATION. THE TWO MOST IMPORTANT WORDS REGARDING PERSONAL SECURITY ARE "PAY ATTENTION'.

IF YOU DO CARRY A HANDGUN AND KNOW HOW TO USE IT, DON'T HESITATE TO DO SO IN THE CASE OF A HOME INVASION, CARJACKING, ATM ROBBERY, MUGGING, OR RANDOM ASSAULT. SHOOT THE SONOFABITCH(S) AND EMPTY THE CLIP. THE POLICE DON'T NEED CONFLICTING POLICE REPORTS AND THE COURTS DON'T NEED MORE CASES.

CRIMINALS USING A WEAPON IN THE COMMISSION OF A CRIME SHOULD BE LOCKED UP FOR A MINIMUM OF TWENTY-FIVE YEARS WITH NO PAROLE. SECOND OFFENDERS WOULD RECEIVE LIFE WITHOUT PAROLE.

[OF COURSE THE PRISON SYSTEM AS WE KNOW IT WILL HAVE TO BE REORGANIZED AND DIRECTED TOWARD A MUCH MORE HUMANE AND THERAPEUTIC APPROACH TO REHABILITATION, BUT THAT'S A WHOLE OTHER ISSUE. SUFFICE IT TO SAY THAT AN ENLIGHTENED PRISON SYSTEM WALKS HAND IN HAND WITH ZERO TOLERANCE SENTENCES, IN OTHER WORDS, GET THEM OFF THE STREETS THEN MAKE MORE THAN A TOKEN EFFORT TO ASSIST EACH PERSON WITH THEIR PERSONAL AND SPIRITUAL GROWTH. FOR EXAMPLE: PHYSICALLY WE CAN HELP THE MALE RAPIST OR CHILD MOLESTER BY CASTRATING HIM AND REMOVING HIS PENIS]

PROSTITUTION:

THE OLDEST PROFESSION IN THE WORLD SHOULD BE LEGALIZED. ACTIVITY SHOULD BE RESTRICTED TO SPECIFIC LOCATIONS AND LICENSED AND REGULATED BY LOCAL HEALTH DEPARTMENTS. A SERVICE TAX SHOULD BE EXACTED WITH EVERY PURCHASE THAT WOULD PAY FOR THE ADMINISTRATION. ONCE THE PROGRAM IS OPERATIONAL, ANY MAN THAT IS CONVICTED OF PIMPING OR PANDERING WILL BE CASTRATED AND FORCED TO PERFORM MAINTENANCE ON THE NEW FACILITIES FOR HOWEVER LONG THE JUDGE DEEMS APPROPRIATE.

RAPISTS AND CHILD MOLESTERS:

RAPISTS, CHILD MOLESTERS, OR ANYONE THAT COMMITS A CRIME OF A SEXUAL NATURE WHETHER IT IS OVERTLY VIOLENT OR NOT SHOULD BE LOCKED UP FOR LIFE WITHOUT PAROLE. MALE PERPETRATORS SHOULD BE CASTRATED. THAT MAY SOUND CRUEL (NOT TO THE VICTIM) BUT IT IS THE MOST HUMANE THING TO DO; REMOVE MUCH OF THE SEX DRIVE AND YOU ALLOW THE POSSIBILITY OF REDIRECTED POSITIVE BEHAVIOR.

IF THE PREDATOR COMMITS MAYHEM (AMPUTATION OF BODY PARTS, DISMEMBERMENT), OR ATTEMPTS TO KILL THE VICTIM, THE CRIME SHOULD BE ELEVATED TO THE CRIMINAL EQUIVALENT OF MURDER ONE AND ADJUDICATED ACCORDINGLY.

EVERY PAROLED SEX OFFENDER SHOULD HAVE TO REGISTER WITH LOCAL LAW ENFORCEMENT WHO IN TURN WOULD HAVE THE OBLIGATION TO NOTIFY MEMBERS OF THE NEIGHBORHOOD AND COMMUNITY OF HIS/HER INTENTION TO RESIDE THERE. LAW ENFORCEMENT WOULD ALSO PROVIDE A PICTURE OF THE PERSON ALONG WITH THEIR ADDRESS.

STALKERS:

FOR SOME MYSTERIOUS REASON, LAW ENFORCEMENT'S STANCE ON STALKERS HAS BEEN OUTRAGEOUSLY UNREALISTIC AND LAX. STALKING IS POTENTIALLY ONE OF THE MOST DISRUPTIVE AND DANGEROUS CRIMINAL PASTIMES IN THE SOCIAL ORDER; MADE SO BECAUSE THE ACTIVITY IS OFTEN MOTIVATED BY IRRATIONAL AND/OR MISDIRECTED PASSION. AS THE CONDUCT CONTINUES, THE EXECUTION OR PHYSICAL MANIFESTATION OF THE OBSESSION MORE OFTEN THAN NOT, BECOMES CRIMINAL.

A WOMAN OR MAN SHOULD NOT HAVE TO OFFER UP EXTRAORDINARY PROOF TO LAW ENFORCEMENT IN ORDER TO GET THEM INVOLVED. STALKING IS TRULY ONE CRIME THAT SHOULD BE ACTED ON AT FIRST MENTION. IT IS NO BIG THING FOR THE ACCUSED TO PROVE THAT HE/SHE IS NOT GUILTY OF THE ALLEGATION WHILE THE WHOLE SAD SITUATION IS SOMEWHAT BENIGN. LETTING IT FESTER AND BURROW CAUSES THE ULTIMATE MALIGNANCY, WHICH IS SOME KIND OF VIOLENT ACT.

DAVID HAYDEN

IF THE ACCUSED APPEARS CULPABLE, THAT PERSON NEEDS TO BE REMANDED TO A FACILITY FOR PSYCHIATRIC EVALUATION AND TREATED IF NEEDED. IF THE STALKER PERSISTS FOLLOWING TREATMENT, THEN THE INDIVIDUAL SHOULD BE LOCKED UP FOR A PERIOD OF TIME AS THE COURT DEEMS APPROPRIATE. IF THE PERSON CONTINUES TO STALK AFTER HIS/HER RELEASE THE FIRST TIME, THE OFFENDER SHOULD BE LOCKED UP FOR LIFE WITHOUT PAROLE.

MURDER:

THE ONLY METHOD OF EXECUTION IN AMERICA SHOULD BE LETHAL INJECTION. THE PROCESS SHOULD NOT BE ACCOMPLISHED IN THE CHICKEN SHIT AND ARCHAIC METHOD CURRENTLY USED. THE IV SHOULDN'T PASS THROUGH A SERIES OF SCREENS AND WALLS, THE ONLY ACCEPTABLE PARTITION WOULD BE SOMETHING SIMILAR TO A SHOJI SCREEN, THUS ELIMINATING ANY ERROR IN ADMINISTRATION THAT IS CAUSED BY THE OBSTRUCTIONS AND DISTANCE.

ANY PERSON WHO COMMITS A MURDER IN WHICH THERE IS ABSOLUTELY AND UNEQUIVOCALLY NO DOUBT OF GUILT I.E. WITNESSED BY NO LESS THAN THREE UNRELATED AND UNACQUAINTED PERSONS, IN COMBINATION WITH INCONTESTABLE PHYSICAL EVIDENCE (DNA SHOULD CARRY THE MOST WEIGHT WHEN BODILY FLUIDS ARE AVAILABLE), A CONFESSION, AND INCLUDES ALL THE ELEMENTS OF HABEAS CORPUS SHOULD RECEIVE ONE JURY TRIAL. WHEN THE GUILTY VERDICT IS RENDERED, THE CONVICTED SHOULD BE SENTENCED TO DEATH BY LETHAL INJECTION WITHIN FORTY-FIVE DAYS OF THE VERDICT.

AN APPELLATE COURT IN THE APPROPRIATE JURISDICTION WILL BE REQUIRED TO REVIEW THE CASE AND TRIAL WITHIN THIRTY DAYS TO ELIMINATE ANY OUTSIDE CHANCE OF CHICANERY. THAT'S IT. NO MORE APPEALS.

I AM SPEAKING ABOVE ABOUT THE MANSON'S, DAHMER'S, BUNDY'S, AND LIKE WHOSE EXISTENCE LACKS ANY SOCIAL VALUE AND IN THE TRUE SENSE OF THE WORD ARE SOCIOPATHS.

THIS INCLUDES PEOPLE WHO KILL DURING "CRIMES OF PASSION" WHICH ARE AGAIN, PHYSICAL EXPRESSIONS OF PURELY ANIMAL BEHAVIOR. THE FACT THAT THE GUILTY PARTIES WERE UNDER THE INFLUENCE OF DRUGS OR ALCOHOL WOULD HAVE NO BEARING IN THE CASE. A PERSON THAT INTRODUCES A PERCEPTION ALTERING SUBSTANCE INTO THEIR SYSTEM SHOULD NOT ESCAPE RESPONSIBILITY FOR HIS/HER ACTIONS.

SANITY WOULD NEVER BE AN ISSUE, SOCIETY IN THE TWENTIETH CENTURY NO LONGER HAS THE LUXURIES OF TIME OR MONEY TO STUDY AND CLINICALLY INVESTIGATE A MURDERER FOR REASONS WHY. THEY NEED TO BE SENT UP TO ANGEL AUTO-BODY FOR REPAIR AND EVENTUAL REINCARNATION.

OTHER THAN THE OBVIOUS (CASES ABOVE), THE JUDICIAL SYSTEM IS TOO FLAWED IN IT'S DISPENSATION OF JUSTICE TO ALLOW FOR THE POSSIBILITY OF ONE INNOCENT PERSON BEING EUTHANIZED.

THOSE ACCUSED OF CAPITAL CRIMES BASED ON CIRCUMSTANTIAL EVIDENCE ARE ENTITLED TO A FULL DOSE OF DUE PROCESS UNDER THE LAW. HOWEVER, THE LEGAL SYSTEM MUST ADOPT A LESS LENIENT POLICY REGARDING PROCEDURAL INFRACTIONS. IF A SUSPECT HAS BEEN FOUND UNANIMOUSLY GUILTY BY TWELVE MEN AND WOMEN, THE CASE SHOULDN'T BE THROWN OUT FOR LACK OF MIRANDA OR ILLEGAL SEARCH AND SEIZURE AS EXAMPLES.

DOMESTIC VIOLENCE:

FOR REFERENCE, THERE ARE APPROXIMATELY 3800 ANIMAL SHELTERS IN THE UNITED STATES. THERE ARE ONLY 1500 SHELTERS OR "SAFE HOUSES" FOR VICTIMS OF SPOUSAL ABUSE OR DOMESTIC VIOLENCE.

A MINIMUM OF TEN MILLION CHILDREN BEAR WITNESS TO DOMESTIC VIOLENCE ANNUALLY.

ANY MAN THAT HITS A WOMAN SHOULD BE LOCKED UP FOR A MINIMUM OF ONE YEAR AND BE REQUIRED TO ATTEND AND PASS A COMPREHENSIVE REHABILITATION COURSE WHILE INCARCERATED AS A CONDITION FOR RELEASE.

SECOND OFFENDERS SHOULD BE LOCKED UP FOR A MINIMUM OF FIVE YEARS WITHOUT POSSIBILITY OF PAROLE. THEIR TIME SHOULD BE SPENT AT A MINIMUM SECURITY FACILITY FROM WHERE THEY LABOR DAILY IN THEIR COMMUNITY ON PROJECTS THAT ADDRESS AND SERVE THE PURPOSE OF PROMOTING THE WELFARE OF ALL WOMEN.

THIRD OFFENDERS SHOULD BE SENT BEFORE A TRIBUNAL COMPOSED ENTIRELY OF EDUCATED WOMEN WHO HAVE BEEN VICTIMS OF MALE ABUSE. THE WOMEN WOULD SOLELY DECIDE, WITH NO POSSIBLE APPEAL, WHAT SENTENCE WOULD BE IMPOSED UPON THE BRUTE.

AIDS:

ANY INDIVIDUAL OF EITHER SEX THAT INTENTIONALLY INTERACTS WITH AN OTHERWISE INNOCENT PERSON IN SUCH A WAY THAT WOULD TRANSMIT THE DISEASE SHOULD BE CHARGED WITH ATTEMPTED MURDER AND IMMEDIATELY REMOVED FROM ALL CONTACT WITH OTHER PEOPLE. IF THE VICTIM DIES THEN THE CARRIER (IF STILL ALIVE) SHOULD BE CHARGED WITH MURDER. THE CARRIER SHOULD SPEND THE REMAINDER OF THEIR LIFE CASTRATED OR STERILIZED, AND IN SOLITARY CONFINEMENT.

REFORM OF LEGAL SYSTEM:

THE CUMBERSOME NATURE OF THE MULTI-TIERED AND COMPLEX CRIMINAL JUSTICE SYSTEM NEEDS TO BE COMPLETELY OVERHAULED, BUT IS FAR TOO MUCH TO TACKLE IN THIS OUTLINE. SUFFICE IT TO SAY, SOME IMMEDIATE CHANGES WOULD HELP AS MENTIONED BELOW.

[CONCURRENT WITH COMMON SENSE, THE ENTIRE JUDICIAL STRUCTURE NEEDS TO BE UNIFIED, STREAMLINED, AND COMPLETELY REMOVED FROM THE POLITICAL PROCESS. A SEPARATE JUDICIAL REVIEW BOARD SHOULD BE ESTABLISHED TO DEAL WITH ALL JUDICIAL APPOINTMENTS, ALONG WITH ALL EVALUATIONS OF PERFORMANCE OF SEATED JUDGES. THE MEMBERS OF THE JUDICIAL REVIEW BOARD SHOULD BE LIMITED TO ONE TEN YEAR

TERM EACH. ADDITIONALLY, NO TENURE ON ANY BENCH SHOULD EXCEED FIFTEEN YEARS.]

PERHAPS THE MOST FLAGRANT EXAMPLE OF THE POLITICAL ABUSE OF POWER WAS BUSH'S NOMINATION OF CLARENCE THOMAS TO THE SUPREME COURT. THOMAS ISN'T QUALIFIED TO SIT ON ANY SEAT OTHER THAN A TOILET SEAT. HE'D NEVER DISTINGUISHED HIMSELF IN ANY WAY AS A TEACHER, AUTHOR, ATTORNEY, OR JUDGE.

WE DO BELIEVE YOU ANITA.

IN CONJUNCTION WITH ECONOMIZING THE COURTHOUSES, LAWYERS INCOMES MUST BE REGULATED. THE HIGH COST OF LITIGATION MUST BE REDUCED SO THAT ALL LIVING BENEATH THE BLINDFOLDED EYES OF LADY JUSTICE HAVE ACCESS TO HER.

IT IS NOT AS IF LAWYERS AND DOCTORS FOR THAT MATTER, CHOSE THEIR RESPECTIVE PROFESSIONS TO PROMOTE THE COMMON GOOD. THE ILLUSION OF ALTRUISM IS JUST THAT, A SMOKESCREEN ESTABLISHED BY THE GREEDY BASTARDS TO BOOST THEIR INCOME AND SOCIAL STANDING.

JAILS:

JAILS ARE A SOCIETY'S PHYSICAL PROOF OF ITS FAILURE TO DESIGN AND MAINTAIN AN EQUITABLE AND RELEVANT INFRASTRUCTURE. IN CONCERT WITH THE REHABILITATION OF THE INSTITUTIONS THEMSELVES, MASSIVE RESOURCES IN THE FORM OF BOTH MONEY AND ENERGY NEED TO BE ALLOCATED AND DIRECTED TO BOTH ACADEMIC AND VOCATIONAL SCHOOLS, TO SOPHISTICATED AND AVAILABLE DRUG REHAB CLINICS, AND TO AFFORDABLE AND/ OR FREE COUNSELING/THERAPEUTIC FACILITIES, BOTH IN HOUSE AND MORE IMPORTANTLY IN OUR CITIES.

THERE ARE THOSE INCOMPLETE HUMAN BEINGS (DEFINITION OF COMPLETE TO INCLUDE A CONSCIENCE AND SENSE OF SOCIAL RESPONSIBILITY) WHO WILL NEVER FIT INTO SOCIETY AND MUST BE PERMANENTLY REMOVED.

THE INSTITUTIONS NEED TO BE HUMANELY ADMINISTERED IN THAT ALL THOSE THINGS THAT SHOULD EXIST IN SOCIETY, HEALTH CARE, NUTRITION, EDUCATION, SAFE ENVIRONMENT, ALONG WITH A SENSE OF FUTURE, DO, PERHAPS OFFERING UP AS AN EXAMPLE TO THOSE BEYOND THE WALLS THAT, IN EVEN LOW DOSES, LIGHT CAN OVERCOME THE DARK.

LOOTERS:

A SEPARATE APPROACH IS TAKEN TOWARD LOOTERS DURING NATURAL CATASTROPHES SUCH AS EARTHQUAKES, FIRES, TSUNAMIS, OR RIOTS. LOOTING IS DISGUSTING AND BASE ANIMAL BEHAVIOR AND SHOULD NEVER BE TOLERATED. DISASTERS OF ANY KIND PROVIDE THE OPPORTUNITY FOR A PEOPLE TO PULL TOGETHER AND RISE ABOVE THE QUAGMIRE AND CONFUSION OF DIFFERENCE AND SEPARATION. THE OLD AXIOM THAT THE BEST OF THE HUMAN SPIRIT CAN BE MOST OFTEN SEEN DURING THE WORST OF TIMES REMAINS TRUE IN EVERY TEST.

"ACTS OF GOD" (WHICH THEY AREN'T) PRESENT THE CLOSEST COMPARISON TO THE CHAOS OF A CIVIL WAR THAN ANY OTHER EVENT. AS SUCH THE RULES OF ENGAGEMENT SHOULD BE SIMILAR.

IF ANY INDIVIDUAL IS EITHER INSIDE OR OUT OF ANOTHER PERSON'S HOME OR BUSINESS DURING ANY NATURAL DISASTER, MAN MADE OR OTHERWISE AND WITH STOLEN PROPERTY IN HAND, THE POLICE, NATIONAL GUARD, OR PROPERTY OWNER HAS AN ABSOLUTE RIGHT TO SHOOT THE THIEF. IF THE ACTION IS EVER QUESTIONED IN ANY ARENA, THE ONLY ISSUE CONCERNING MISCONDUCT WILL BE WHETHER THE SLAIN OR WOUNDED SUSPECT HAD POSSESSION OF STOLEN PROPERTY.

DNA:

ALL PERSONS FOUND GUILTY OF ANY KIND OF CRIME SHOULD BE REQUIRED TO PROVIDE A DNA SAMPLE TO A NATIONAL BANK.

DEADBEAT DADS AND MOMS

"MEN WILL ROUTINELY SPEND MORE TIME CARING FOR THEIR CAR THAN THEY WILL ON THEIR CHILD"

TWO MILLION COUPLES DIVORCE ANNUALLY LEAVING ONE MILLION KIDS IN THE LURCH. IT IS IMPORTANT TO REMEMBER THAT THE DECISION TO HAVE CHILDREN IMPACTS EVERYONE IN SOCIETY IN SOME WAY.

THE ONLY ISSUE HERE IS THE TAKING OF AND/OR ACCEPTING RESPONSIBILITY FOR OUR BEHAVIOR.

ANY ANIMAL CAN IMPREGNATE OR BEAR A CHILD. THERE'S NOTHING TO IT. IT IS NO RICH ACCOMPLISHMENT MERITING THE PASSING OUT OF CIGARS (WHY CELEBRATE LIFE WITH DEATH?) OR THUMPING ON THE CHEST. WHAT IS AN ACCOMPLISHMENT IS BECOMING AND BEING A CAPABLE AND CARING PARENT. ANYONE CAN HAVE A KID BUT NOT EVERYONE CAN PARENT.

MEN ROUTINELY WILL SPEND MORE TIME CARING FOR THEIR CAR THAN THEY WILL ON THEIR CHILD. THE VERY LEAST A PARENT CAN DO FOR THEIR CHILD IS TO PROVIDE THE FINANCIAL SUPPORT NECESSARY TO INSURE THEIR CHILD HAS AT MINIMUM THE MONEY FOR FOOD, HEALTH CARE, CLOTHING, SHELTER, AND EDUCATION. IN THE 1990'S THE COST ESTIMATE FOR THAT EXCEEDS $125,000 DURING THE FIRST EIGHTEEN YEARS OF A CHILD'S LIFE.

IF A MOTHER AND FATHER ARE ENTRENCHED IN THE WELFARE SYSTEM (HUD, FOOD STAMPS, MEDICARE, ATD, ETC.) AND DEMONSTRATE NO DESIRE TO FEND FOR THEMSELVES, THEY ARE BY VIRTUE OF THEIR SITUATION QUESTIONABLY FIT PARENTS. THE CHILDREN IN THAT KIND OF LIVING ENVIRONMENT WILL ONLY HAVE ACCESS TO THE BASICS PROVIDING BOTH ADULTS AREN'T SUBSTANCE ABUSERS AND BOTH ASSUME PARENTING ROLES.

REGARDLESS OF IT ALL, THE TWO CHILD RULE MUST APPLY. IF EITHER THE MAN OR WOMAN HAS HAD TWO CHILDREN TOGETHER OR IN OTHER LIAISONS, THEY MUST AGREE TO TEMPORARY STERILIZATION WHILE ON WELFARE. IF EITHER IS INVOLVED IN

THE CREATION OF A THIRD CHILD PRIOR TO THE PROCEDURE, THE STERILIZATION WILL BE PERMANENT. IF THE HOME IS UNFIT, THE CHILDREN WILL BE REMOVED TO A MORE NURTURING HOME AND THE COUPLE'S BENEFITS WILL BE ACCORDINGLY REDUCED.

ANY DIVORCED DAD WHO REFUSES TO PAY HIS COURT ORDERED MONTHLY CHILD SUPPORT WILL BE LOCATED AND APPREHENDED AND ONE OR ALL OF SEVERAL SANCTIONS WILL BE LEVIED AGAINST HIM. HE MAY BE DENIED A DRIVERS LICENSE UNTIL HE BECOMES CURRENT, HE MAY BE FINED TWICE THE ORIGINAL AMOUNT, IF HE'S A FLIGHT RISK, HE MAY BE INCARCERATED DURING THE TIME IT TAKES TO SEIZE ALL OF HIS ASSETS, AND IF HE HAS ALREADY BROUGHT TWO CHILDREN INTO THE WORLD, HE WILL BE STERILIZED.

THE SAME RULES APPLY EQUALLY TO DEADBEAT MOM'S.

ALL OF THE INVESTIGATIONS REQUIRED TO LOCATE AND ARREST EITHER DEADBEAT WILL BE DONE BY PRIVATE INVESTIGATORS UNDER GOVERNMENT CONTRACT. THEIR COST WILL BE ADDED ON TO THE AMOUNT ALREADY OWED BY THE DELINQUENT DAD OR MOM. SOCIAL SERVICES NEED TO GET OUT OF THE P.I. BUSINESS AND THE COPS DON'T HAVE TIME.

IF EITHER A MAN OR A WOMAN HAS MORE CHILDREN WITH DIFFERENT MATES, HE/SHE WILL BE STERILIZED.

BRINGING AN UNWANTED CHILD, A CHILD THAT IS EXPOSED TO SUBSTANCE ABUSE DURING PREGNANCY, A CHILD THAT DOES NOT RECEIVE PROPER PRE-NATAL CARE, OR A CHILD BORN INTO AN ENVIRONMENT ABSENT OF RESOURCES TO EVEN MINIMALLY PROVIDE CARE IS AN ABUSED CHILD. THE MOTHER AND/OR FATHER OF THAT CHILD WILL BE AT LEAST TEMPORARILY IF NOT PERMANENTLY STERILIZED. THE CHILD WILL BE REMOVED TO A HEALTHIER HOME AND THE PARENTS ASSETS IF ANY, WILL BE SEIZED TO PAY FOR THE RELOCATION AND CONTINUED SUPPORT.

DOMESTIC PARTNERS

"GAY COUPLES SHOULD BE ALLOWED TO MARRY AND
RECEIVE ALL OF THE SOCIAL AND LEGAL BENEFIT OF THAT
UNION"

EVERY SPECIES OF ANIMAL IN THE KINGDOM INCLUDES BOTH
HETEROSEXUAL AND HOMOSEXUAL MEMBERS.

THE PREDOMINATELY STRAIGHT PEOPLE PERFORM THAT BASIC
FUNCTION WHICH IS ESSENTIAL TO PROPAGATION OF THE CLASS,
THAT IS TO REPRODUCE, AND REPRODUCE THEY DO. ALL OTHER LIFE
FORM'S NUMBERS ARE REGULATED BY A TERM WHOSE MEANING
HAS DIMINISHED CONSIDERABLY SINCE THE RELATIVELY RECENT
DOMINATION OF MAN; THE BALANCE OF NATURE.

WITH THE EXCEPTION OF THE WASP'S (WHITE ANGLO SAXON
PROTESTANTS OR EURO-MALES), MOST OTHER ANIMAL FAMILY'S
ACCEPT THEIR HOMOSEXUAL BRETHREN. ONLY IN AMERICA
ARE GAY PEOPLE ATTACKED AND OSTRACIZED, PRIMARILY BY
PRACTITIONERS OF THE RELIGIOUS WRONG WHOSE AGENDA IS NOT
DISSIMILAR TO THAT OF THE DISCIPLES.

THE AUTHORS OF THE BIBLE, DEDICATED SERVANTS ALL,
IMPOSED THEIR OPINIONS AND SELF SERVING PROGNOSTICATIONS
ON THE CURIOUS AND WELL INTENTIONED SEEKERS OF SPIRITUAL
TRUTH, AND IN DOING SO, ELIMINATED ANY ACTUAL ASSOCIATION
WITH JESUS. AS SUPPORT, THE ERRANT EVANGELISTS SAY, "LOOK,
IT SAYS SO IN THE BIBLE". WE ALL ARE FAMILIAR WITH THE HYMN
"HOW DO I KNOW? THE BIBLE TELLS ME SO".

THE BIBLE IS JUST A BOOK WRITTEN BY TWELVE DIFFERENT
PEOPLE WITH A COMMON THEME. THEY COULD VERY LIKELY IN THE
CONTEXT OF THE NEW CULT OR ORDER BE SIMILAR TO ASPIRING
BUREAUCRATS OR POLITICIANS, DRIVEN BY EGO AND THE DESIRE
FOR FAVOR, ACCORDINGLY, THEIR TEXT REFLECTS THAT AMBITION
AND SUBJECTIVE TEXT.

OR IN THIS CASE, BIBLE THUMPERS AND BUREAUCRATS DETERMINED TO IMPOSE THEIR IGNORANCE AND BULLSHIT ON LOVE.

IT IS PREPOSTEROUS, ARCHAIC, AND SPIRITUALLY VACUOUS TO RESTRICT OR LIMIT THE BEHAVIOR OF TWO HUMAN BEINGS IN LOVE.

ANY COUPLE, REGARDLESS OF GENDER, THAT TRULY RESPECTS, LOVES, AND DESIRES TO SPEND THEIR LIVES TOGETHER SHOULD BE ALLOWED TO LEGALLY MARRY AND ENJOY ALL THE BENEFITS SOCIETY OFFERS A LEGALLY WED PAIR.

MARRIED GAY COUPLES CERTAINLY COULDN'T DO ANY WORSE THAN HETEROSEXUAL COUPLES IN TERMS OF DIVORCE, CHILD NEGLECT AND ABUSE, AND GENERALLY IRRESPONSIBLE BEHAVIOR.

WE ALL HAVE OUR PERSONAL OPINIONS AND PATHS DEFINED IN LARGE PART BY THE WRECKAGE AND LUGGAGE IN OUR LIVES. IT IS ONLY IN OUR ABILITY TO FAIRLY AND HONESTLY DEAL WITH OUR PAIN AND INSECURITY THAT WE CAN HOPE TO DIVORCE OURSELVES FROM THE NEED TO LASH OUT AND CONTROL THAT IN OTHERS WHICH WE CANNOT CONTROL IN OURSELVES.

THE TRULY ENLIGHTENED WILL OVERCOME PERSONAL PREFERENCE IN DEFERENCE TO THE COMMON GOOD.

THERE SHOULD BE NO SEPARATION OR DISTINCTION IN LAW BETWEEN GAY AND STRAIGHT COUPLES.

THIS INCLUDES CONSIDERATION OF EMPLOYMENT, MILITARY SERVICE, GOVERNMENT SERVICE, EMPLOYEE BENEFITS, INSURANCE, AND CREDIT OR PURCHASING.

GAY COUPLES SHOULD BE ALLOWED TO MARRY AND RECEIVE ALL OF THE SOCIAL AND LEGAL RECOGNITION AND BENEFIT OF THAT UNION.

IF SO DESIRED, THEY SHOULD BE ENCOURAGED TO ADOPT AND RAISE CHILDREN.

VICTIMS OF A GENDER RELATED HATE CRIME (GAY BASHING) SHOULD BE ENCOURAGED TO SEEK COMPENSATION IN CIVIL COURT. PARENTS OF MINORS WILL BE HELD ABSOLUTELY LIABLE FOR THE CONDUCT OF THEIR CHILDREN. DAMAGES AWARDED SHOULD BE EXCESSIVE AND INVOLVE SEIZURE OF ASSETS. ONLY WHEN THE HATEFUL HUMAN ANIMAL UNDERSTANDS THAT CIVIL RIGHTS VIOLATIONS OF ANY KIND WILL ABSOLUTELY NOT BE TOLERATED CAN WE EXPECT AT LEAST ITS OVERT EXPRESSION TO DISAPPEAR.

DRUGS

"THE MOMENT HARD EVIDENCE EMERGED TESTIFYING TO THE DANGERS INHERENT IN BOTH FIRST AND SECOND HAND SMOKE, ANY OF THE INDUSTRY'S REAL OR IMAGINED RIGHTS CEASED TO EXIST"

HARD STUFF:

IT IS TRAGIC THAT NOT EVERYONE GOT A FAIR AND EVEN SHAKE BY VIRTUE OF BIRTH OR GENETIC CIRCUMSTANCE, BUT A SOCIAL SYSTEM CANNOT TOLERATE, EVEN IN THE NAME OF SYMPATHY AND UNDERSTANDING, BEING ATTACKED AND MUGGED BY MEMBERS OF THE COMMUNITY WHO HAVE OPTED TO BECOME PREDATORS TO SUPPORT THEIR HABIT.

WHAT IS EQUALLY DISTURBING IN THE FINAL YEARS OF THE TWENTIETH CENTURY IS THAT THE DISPENSATION OF "JUSTICE" IS ANYTHING BUT FAIR. WEALTHY OR "CONNECTED" WHITE FOLKS ROUTINELY PURCHASE AND USE COCAINE ALONG WITH A HOST OF OTHER "DESIGNER" DRUGS WITH LITTLE OR NO INTERFERENCE FROM THE LAW WHILE POOR PEOPLE AND PEOPLE OF COLOR (TWO OFTEN KINDRED SPIRITS) RECEIVE MEGA-DOSES OF SUSPICION, SURVEILLANCE, AND APPREHENSION FOR MINUTE QUANTITIES OF CRACK OR CRYSTAL METH AS ONLY TWO OF MANY EXAMPLES.

IT'S ALL ABOUT WHAT ONE CAN AFFORD.

IN THE MICROCOSM, THE INDIVIDUAL RELEGATED BY FATE AND CIRCUMSTANCE TO THE CELLAR OF THE SOCIAL ORDER, IS RESTRICTED TO DRUGS THAT ARE CHEAP AND OFTEN UNSAFE. IN THE MACROCOSM, THE SOCIAL PYRAMID BY DESIGN PROVIDES A CLEAR ILLUSTRATION OF PARALLEL DISPARITY CONCERNING THE PURCHASE OF ANY GOOD OR SERVICE ON THE MARKET.

THE WEALTHY WILL SHOP WITHOUT SCRUTINY AT THE FINEST STORES. IF THEY SO DESIRE, THEY ACCESS THE FINEST DRUGS. THEY CAN AFFORD SECRET AND INSULATED LIVES.

THE MIDDLE INCOME AND POOR ON THE PYRAMID ARE FORCED TO OPERATE IN THE "OPEN", ILLUMINATED BY THE FLOODLIGHTS OF LEGAL SCRUTINY AND VICTIMIZED BY CRIMINAL CODES WRITTEN BY RICH WHITE GUYS THAT ARE RIDDLED WITH HYPOCRISY AND INJUSTICE.

WHAT TO DO ABOUT IT.

DRUGS SUCH AS COCAINE, METH-AMPHETAMINES, ACID, SYNTHETIC "UPPERS" AND "DOWNERS", ALONG WITH THE NEW CLASS OF "DESIGNER" DRUGS SHOULD BE ILLEGAL TO MANUFACTURE, IMPORT, DISTRIBUTE, AND/OR SELL. ENFORCEMENT FOCUS SHOULD BE ON THE SUPPLY ASPECTS OF THE PROBLEM. DOMESTICALLY, ANYONE CAUGHT AND CONVICTED OF MANUFACTURING SYNTHETIC DRUGS WILL NOT ONLY GO TO JAIL, BUT THEY WILL HAVE ALL OF THEIR ASSETS SEIZED TO DEFRAY THE COSTS INCURRED IN THEIR CONVICTION AND INCARCERATION.

THE PEOPLE WHO DIRECTLY RECEIVE THE IMPORTED DRUGS FROM OTHER COUNTRIES (HEROIN, COCAINE) WILL SUFFER THE SAME PENALTY AS THOSE MENTIONED ABOVE WITH EMPHASIS ONCE AGAIN, OF TOTAL LOSS OF PERSONAL PROPERTY AND FREEDOM.

IF ANY OF THE CRIMINAL ACTIVITY IS CONDUCTED AROUND CHILDREN, THE KIDS WILL BE REMOVED FROM THE ENVIRONMENT AND THE PARENTS WILL BE STERILIZED.

ALCOHOL:

IF A PERSON GETS CAUGHT DRUNK DRIVING, HE/SHE WILL LOSE THEIR LICENSE FOR ONE YEAR. IF AT ANY TIME IN THE REMAINDER OF HIS/HER LIFE HE/SHE IS FOUND GUILTY OF ANOTHER DRUNK DRIVING OFFENCE, THEIR DRIVING PRIVILEGE WILL BE REVOKED PERMANENTLY WITHOUT APPEAL AND THE FINE WILL BUMP TO $10,000 WHICH CAN BE RETRIEVED FROM ASSETS.

ANY PERSON THAT CAUSES THE DEATH OF ANOTHER WHILE LEGALLY DRUNK WILL BE CHARGED WITH MURDER IN THE FIRST DEGREE. IT IS QUITE PROPER AND REASONABLE TO ASSUME IF THE ALCOHOL WERE ABSENT FROM THE SYSTEM, THE DEATH WOULD NOT HAVE OCCURRED.

PARENTS OF UNDERAGE DRINKERS SHOULD BE FINANCIALLY RESPONSIBLE FOR THEIR CHILD'S CONDUCT. IF RESPONSIBLE PARENTING IS UNAVAILABLE, THE CHILD WILL BE RELOCATED TO A BETTER AND MORE NURTURING ENVIRONMENT. PARENTS THAT ARE BASICALLY SHITBIRDS WILL BE STERILIZED AND WHAT ASSETS THEY HAVE WILL BE USED TO PAY FOR THE PROCESS.

IMPORTED CROPS:

CROPS THAT ARE GROWN IN CENTRAL AND SOUTH AMERICA, THE MIDDLE EAST, SOUTHEAST ASIA, EUROPE, OR ANYWHERE BEYOND OUR BORDERS SHOULD BE DESTROYED BY AGGRESSIVE MILITARY ACTION. IT'S AN ABSOLUTE JOKE TO ASSUME THAT ANY MONEY SENT TO COUNTRIES LIKE MEXICO OR COLUMBIA (AS EXAMPLES) FOR DRUG PREVENTION WILL NOT END UP IN THE POCKET OF SOME POLITICO. THE BILLIONS THAT WE DO WASTE ANNUALLY SHOULD BE REDIRECTED INTERNALLY TO DRUG REHAB AND SELF START PROGRAMS. THE CROPS CAN BE LOCATED USING ULTRA SENSITIVE SATELLITES, AND THEY CAN AND SHOULD BE DESTROYED FROM THE AIR. NO GROUND TROOPS SHOULD BE INVOLVED. ADVANCE NOTICE SHOULD BE GIVEN TO THE OFFENDING COUNTRY TO MINIMIZE LOSS OF LIFE, THAT WITHIN A CERTAIN AMOUNT OF HOURS SPECIFIC LAND MASSES AND/OR BUILDINGS WILL CEASE TO EXIST AND IF THEY DON'T LIKE THAT MUSIC AND WANT TO DANCE, THEY'D BETTER BRING THEIR BEST SHOES.

EPIDEMICS NEED TO BE TREATED AS SUCH.

MARIJUANA AND RELATIVES:

MARIJUANA, HASH, AND OPIUM SHOULD BE LEGALIZED AND THEIR USE SHOULD BE RESTRICTED TO FACILITIES SIMILAR TO "OPIUM DENS" WHERE CERTAIN SOCIETAL SAFEGUARDS COULD BE FOLLOWED. INHERENT IN THIS WHOLE APPROACH IS THAT SPECIFIC GIVE AND TAKE IS REQUIRED. IF ONE CHOOSES TO FREQUENT SUCH AN ESTABLISHMENT, HE/SHE HAD BETTER BE READY TO FORFEIT PROPAGATION, HAD BETTER BE ABLE TO AFFORD THE "TRIP", HAVE HAD MADE NECESSARY TRAVEL ARRANGEMENTS TO AND FROM, AND BE WILLING TO SUBMIT TO IN HOUSE DRUG TESTS PAID FOR

BY THE MEMBERSHIP FEES. ALL FACILITIES WOULD BE NON-PROFIT AND CAREFULLY REGULATED AGAINST SAME.

PHARMACEUTICAL INDUSTRY:

AMERICA IS MEDICATED AND BEING RIPPED OFF IN THE PROCESS. IN CONCERT WITH PHYSICIANS, THE PHARMACEUTICAL INDUSTRY HAS OPERATED IN A GLOBAL ARENA WITH VERY LITTLE REGULATION. PREYING ON PAIN AND IGNORANCE, THE ALLIANCE HAS MADE ENORMOUS AMOUNTS OF MONEY DECLARING TO ALL WHO QUESTION CHEMICAL COSTS THAT FUNDING RESEARCH AND DEVELOPMENT IS THE REASON.

WE ALL KNOW THAT'S BULLSHIT. SIMPLE MATH ILLUSTRATES THE POINT.

SUPPOSE VALIUM COST 50 MILLION TO DEVELOP. EASILY ONE HUNDRED MILLION PEOPLE HAVE PAID FOR PRESCRIPTIONS AT A MINIMUM OF TEN BUCKS. THAT'S A BILLION DOLLARS FOLKS. NOT ALL RESEARCH PANS OUT, SO WHAT HAPPENED TO RISK IN THE FREE ENTERPRISE SYSTEM? NOT ONLY THAT, THE PHARMACEUTICAL COMPANY'S ARE ALLOWED TO WRITE OFF MUCH OF THEIR LOSS AT THE END OF THE YEAR, BESIDES RECEIVING OUR TAX MONEY FOR THEIR R&D. IT'S COMPLETELY CORRUPT AND OUT OF WHACK.

THE PHARMACEUTICAL INDUSTRY SHOULD BE TREATED IN EVERY RESPECT LIKE ANY OTHER COMPANY. THEY SHOULD GENERATE THEIR OWN MONEY FOR R&D, SHOULD NOT BE ALLOWED ANY WRITE OFFS SAVE THOSE COMMON TO ANY BUSINESS SUCH AS DEPRECIATION, AND BE REQUIRED TO PRICE THEIR PRODUCTS BASED ON A FAIR COST PLUS PROFIT RATIO DETERMINED BY ACTUAL R&D, AND PRODUCTION EXPENDITURES.

SINCE LOBBYING IS A FELONY IN MY WORLD, THAT ACTIVITY WOULD CEASE TO EXIST.

THE ONLY TAX REVENUE USED TO ASSIST IN THE R&D PHASES OF PRESCRIPTION AND OVER THE COUNTER DRUGS WOULD BE IN THE CASE OF A NATIONAL EMERGENCY SUCH AS AIDS, AND THEN UNDER CAREFUL SCRUTINY.

Last but not least, the cost of all drugs should be uniform throughout the U.S. and the rest of the world. Codeine should cost the same in London as it does in Louisiana, the same in Texarkana as in Tempe, the same in Scarsdale as in South Central L.A.

All prescription drugs should be considered free trade items immune from tariffs or other economic influences.

As stated in the Preface, my solutions will be general and brief. I have formulated specific plans on how best to accomplish the reorganization, or removal of institutions or policies. Those are better left for another time.

Tobacco:

Seven million kids live in houses where at least one adult smokes, and second hand smoke is twenty-two times more lethal than that which is originally inhaled.

Tobacco is a deadly drug. There is no question in any rational person's mind that nicotine is a carcinogen. It is a toxic and terminal substance that serves no purpose whatsoever in the world save killing all life forms.

The government subsidizes the tobacco industry while spending millions on anti-tobacco advertisements. Those legislators who voted for subsidies should be impeached and incarcerated.

Past decisions and legislation serve only to illustrate mistakes made in America's perception of and approach to a drug in the absence of any scientific data. The only way to chart a new course on a nicotine free sea is to eliminate any and all of the drug's related activity in the United States by Federal Law.

The Industry will cry foul. They will insist that they have the constitutional right to market and provide death not only in America, but in those "new" markets located in countries we so often refer to as "third world".

THEIR CEO'S WILL FURTHER INSIST THAT THEY HAVE THE RIGHT TO LOBBY (SYNONYMOUS WITH BEING BOUGHT OR PURCHASED) ELECTED OFFICIALS AND NO ONE CAN STOP THEM.

I SAY THAT THEY HAVEN'T THE RIGHT TO DO SHIT! THE MOMENT HARD EVIDENCE EMERGED TESTIFYING TO THE DANGERS INHERENT IN BOTH FIRST AND SECOND HAND SMOKE, ANY OF THE INDUSTRY'S REAL OR IMAGINED RIGHTS CEASED TO EXIST.

THE VARIOUS MEMBERS OF THIS INSIDIOUS INDUSTRY SHOULD BE GIVEN THREE YEARS TO GET OUT OF THE BUSINESS. WHETHER THEY CHOOSE TO PLANT A DISSIMILAR SOCIALLY HEALTHY CROP, INVEST OR ACQUIRE OTHER LEGITIMATE COMPANIES, OR SELL THEIR PLANTS (BUILDINGS) AND FIELDS, MAKES NO DIFFERENCE AS LONG AS THE TOBACCO INDUSTRY DISAPPEARS.

THE CORPORATE SOCIOPATHS THAT RUN THE INSTITUTIONS SHOULD RECEIVE NO INCENTIVES, TAX BREAKS, OR FINANCIAL ASSISTANCE OF ANY KIND IN LIEU OF AVOIDING MULTIPLE MURDER CHARGES. IF THEY ATTEMPT TO SELL OFF EVERYTHING AND SPREAD THE MONEY AROUND AMONG THE BOARD'S OF DIRECTORS AND SHAREHOLDERS, ALL OFFICERS SHOULD HAVE ALL OF THEIR PERSONAL ASSETS SEIZED AND BE INCARCERATED FOR LIFE. REGARDLESS, THE COMPANIES WILL BE FORCED TO PAY ALL COSTS RELATIVE TO THE REHABILITATION OF THOSE ADDICTED TO NICOTINE (VARIOUS THERAPIES TO "KICK THE HABIT") IN ADDITION TO REIMBURSING ALL FIFTY STATES FOR HEALTH EXPENDITURES ASSOCIATED WITH NICOTINE RELATED DISEASES.

CONFIDENT THAT THE COMPANIES WILL CONTINUE TO RELOCATE IN OTHER LESS DEVELOPED COUNTRIES, THERE WILL ACCORDINGLY BE NO IMPORTATION OF NICOTINE PRODUCTS. THOSE INDIVIDUALS CAUGHT ATTEMPTING TO OR ACTUALLY CONDUCTING ILLICIT BUSINESS WITHIN THE UNITED STATES BORDERS WILL BE CHARGED WITH MURDER IN THE FIRST DEGREE AND ALL THEIR ASSETS AND PROPERTY WILL BE SEIZED. THEY WILL BE VIEWED BY THE JUDICIAL SYSTEM AS SERIAL KILLERS.

THOSE CITIZENS WHO SOLICIT CONTRABAND TOBACCO PRODUCTS WILL BE CHARGED WITH A FELONY AND WILL HAVE

WHATEVER ASSETS THEY HAVE AVAILABLE SEIZED IN LIEU OF THE PROJECTED COLLECTIVE HEALTH COSTS RELATED NOT ONLY TO PRIMARY, BUT ALSO SECOND HAND SMOKE.

THERE WILL BE NO "NICOTINE POLICE". THERE WILL ALWAYS BE THOSE ANIMALS WHO INSIST ON POLLUTING THEMSELVES AND THE WORLD IN THE NAME OF FREEDOM. SINCE SMOKING OR CHEWING OF ANY KIND WILL BE ILLEGAL ANYWHERE IN THE UNITED STATES, THOSE UNFORTUNATE CREATURES WILL BE FORCED TO HIDE AND SCURRY ABOUT WHILE THEY CONDUCT THEIR CLANDESTINE BUSINESS, MUCH IN THE MANNER A RODENT MIGHT, ASHAMED OF IT'S EXISTENCE YET TOO WEAK TO CHANGE.

EVENTUALLY THE SOCIAL PRESSURE WILL RELIEVE LAW ENFORCEMENT OF MUCH OF THE NEED TO EVEN POLICE THE PROBLEM.

AFTER THE BAN, IF AN INDIVIDUAL IS SEEN SMOKING, A ONE HUNDRED DOLLAR MISDEMEANOR TICKET WILL BE ISSUED. THE SECOND CITATION WILL BUMP THE FINE UP TO $1,000 AND THE THIRD CITATION WOULD COST THE PERP $10,000, AN EXPENSIVE SMOKE AND A REAL DRAG.

OTHER THAN ISSUING CITATIONS, LAW ENFORCEMENT WILL BE OUT OF THE LOOP. THE FIRST AND SECOND CITATIONS WILL BE RECORDED IN THE APPROPRIATE STATE REVENUE OR TAX OFFICE AND BE LISTED AS A REAL DEBT IF NOT PAID. FAILURE TO SATISFY THE DEBT WITHIN ONE CALENDAR YEAR WOULD LEAD TO SANCTIONS SUCH AS LOSS OF DRIVER'S LICENSES ALONG WITH EXCLUSION FROM VOTING (SECOND CITATION FELONS). AT BOTH THE SECOND AND THIRD CITATION LEVEL SEIZURE OF PERSONAL PROPERTY SUCH AS AUTOMOBILES AND REAL ESTATE WOULD BE A STATED AND PUBLICIZED CONSEQUENCE OF FAILURE TO PAY THE FINES. NOBODY WOULD GO TO JAIL.

THE CHILDREN OF PARENTS WHO SMOKE WILL BE REMOVED FROM THE HOME AND PLACED IN A HEALTHIER ENVIRONMENT. THE OFFENDING PARENTS WILL PAY FOR THE PROCESS BY FORFEITING SUFFICIENT CASH OR ASSETS.

PARENTS WHO CONTINUE TO SMOKE AND PUMP OUT CHILDREN WILL BE STERILIZED. AT ANY RATE, IF EITHER SEPARATELY OR TOGETHER THEY'VE BROUGHT TWO CHILDREN INTO THE WORLD (THE MAXIMUM FOR ANY COUPLE IN AMERICA), THAN CAUSE THE PREGNANCY OF A THIRD, PERMANENT STERILIZATION WOULD OCCUR TO BOTH.

EDUCATION

"ADMINISTRATIVE POSITIONS HAVE BECOME POLITICAL
PLUMS RATHER THAN ACTUAL WORKING JOBS.
ADMINISTRATION SALARIES SHOULD BE CAPPED AND NOT
EXCEED FIFTEEN PER CENT MORE THAN THE HIGHEST PAID
TEACHER IN THE STATE"

WITHOUT EXCEPTION, THE KEY TO ANY CIVILIZATIONS SUCCESS IS
BASED IN ITS SYSTEM OF EDUCATION YET, SCHOOL BOND MEASURES
ROUTINELY FAIL TO PASS IN EVERY COMMUNITY IN AMERICA.

THE UNITED STATE'S STUDENTS ALSO FINISH IN THE BOTTOM
THIRD OF ALL THOSE TESTED AMONG SO CALLED DEVELOPED
COUNTRIES. THAT SHOULD COME AS NO SURPRISE. FAMILY UNITS
(LESS THAN FIFTY PER CENT OF MARRIAGES LAST) AND CITIES ARE
FALLING APART. PUBLIC SCHOOLS HAVE BECOME NOTHING MORE
THAN HOLDING COMPANIES ATTEMPTING DAILY TO CONTROL THE
CONFUSION COURSING THROUGH OUR YOUNG ONE'S RAPIDLY
CHANGING HEARTS AND MINDS.

HUMAN RIGHTS ABUSES AND IMITATION ASIDE, ONE HAS TO
LOOK NO FURTHER THAN CHINA AND JAPAN TO WITNESS THE
REWARDS OF A GOOD EDUCATION. THEIR STUDENTS FREELY
TRAVEL INTERNATIONALLY GARNERING THE BEST JOBS AVAILABLE.
THEY ARE IN INCREASING NUMBERS HEADS OF UNIVERSITIES,
CORPORATIONS, AND GOVERNMENT. THERE IS A REASON FOR THAT.
AS STUDENTS THESE PEOPLE WERE PROVIDED AN EXCELLENT
EDUCATION THAT WHEN COMBINED WILL A DILIGENT WORK ETHIC,
PAID OFF IN AN ABILITY TO PERFORM AT HIGH LEVELS.

IN ALL FAIRNESS, WE AMERICANS HAVE HAD MORE THAN OUR
SHARE OF CULTURAL OBSTACLES CONSIDERING OUR LIMITED
INTELLECTUAL AND SPIRITUAL ABILITY TO DEAL WITH THEM.
CHINA, JAPAN, AND THE MIDDLE EAST ARE ALL HOMOGENOUS
SOCIETIES. INTERNALLY, THEY HAVEN'T BEEN DISTRACTED BY
OTHER CULTURES OR PEOPLE THAT LOOK DIFFERENT. THE CITIZENS
OF THESE COUNTRIES ALSO LIVE IN A POLITICAL SYSTEM THAT IS
FAR LESS LENIENT THAN OURS. ALL THAT NOTWITHSTANDING, THE

OTHER COUNTRIES HAVE MANAGED TO AVOID BEING DISTRACTED FROM THE TASK OF EDUCATING.

WE NEED TO ATTACK THE RENOVATION OF OUR SCHOOL SYSTEMS WITH THE PASSION OF A MILITARY MISSION.

NEW SCHOOLS NEED TO BE BUILT. THEY NEED TO BE CONSTRUCTED IN SAFE AND ACCESSIBLE LOCATIONS. THE CLASSROOMS SHOULD BE LARGE, THE CLASSES SMALL. ALL OF THE VOCATIONAL TOOLS OF THE FUTURE MUST BE AVAILABLE TO EVERY STUDENT I.E. COMPUTERS, SCIENCE AND LAB EQUIPMENT, AND MULTIPLE LANGUAGE OPPORTUNITY. [IT WOULD SEEM REASONABLE THAT COMPUTER COMPANIES WOULD EITHER WANT TO DONATE OR SELL AT COST ITS PRODUCT KNOWING FULL WELL THAT THE STUDENTS AS ADULTS WOULD REPRESENT PRIMARY CUSTOMERS]

TEACHERS NEED TO BE BETTER TRAINED AND CONSEQUENTLY, PAID MORE. AS THE MINIMUM WAGE SHOULD BE RAISED IMMEDIATELY, SO SHOULD THERE BE A MINIMUM NATIONAL TEACHING WAGE. PUBLIC SCHOOL INSTRUCTORS SHOULD ALSO BE PROVIDED THE FULL RANGE OF BENEFITS FROM HEALTH CARE TO 401K's.

THE SIZE OF THE SCHOOL ADMINISTRATION SHOULD REFLECT NEED. CURRENTLY, TOO MUCH MONEY IS BEING SPENT ON ADMINISTRATION WITH VERY LITTLE RETURN IN TERMS OF BENEFIT TO OUR STUDENTS. ADMINISTRATION POSITIONS HAVE BECOME POLITICAL PLUMS RATHER THAN ACTUAL WORKING JOBS. ADMINISTRATION SALARIES SHOULD BE CAPPED AND NOT EXCEED FIFTEEN PER CENT MORE THAN THE HIGHEST PAID TEACHER IN THE STATE.

ALL STUDENTS SHOULD BE REQUIRED TO WEAR UNIFORMS UP TO AND INCLUDING THE TWELFTH GRADE. NO STUDENTS WOULD BE ALLOWED TO WEAR BODY PIERCING OR TATTOOS (OF ANY KIND). IF THE INDIVIDUALS SO DESIRE, THEY CAN DO ALL THEY WANT TO THEIR BODIES ONCE THEY GRADUATE FROM HIGH SCHOOL. WHILE THEY ARE IN SCHOOL, THEIR PRIMARY FOCUS SHOULD BE ON GETTING AN EDUCATION WITHOUT THE DISTRACTION OF HAVING TO MAINTAIN A POPULAR OR PEER DRIVEN "LOOK".

It should be noted that by the most conservative estimates, 5,000 teachers are physically assaulted by students in America's schools each day. Parents should be held financially responsible for their child's behavior and liable in civil court.

No public money will be used for private schools. If parents wish to send their kids to a private school, that is their right. Private schools will be taxed as businesses with deductions similar to those allowed churches (see in chapter on taxes). We have to create a new educational environment that is so "cool" and efficient that there would be no more perceived need for private schools. They exist in truth for two reasons, a failed public system, and elitism.

Environment/Mother Earth

"The animal, self named Human, collectively has become an ever expanding skid mark on History's underwear"
Stinky Alfredo

Planet Earth is a pregnant, living entity. Its purpose at this time in cosmic evolution is to support ALL forms of life, from the microscopic single celled organism to the mania known as man. I am certain that in the galactic scheme of things, Earth's existence serves other functions, but than these are beyond human comprehension.

Suffice it to say that it wouldn't be a stretch to draw an analogy between our inner organs as life support and Earth's identical contribution to our survival. If one could imagine the planet covered in all it's circumference at every longitude and latitude with teeming life, then to consider Earth as an internal life sustaining instrument should be easily visualized and understood.

In reality we abuse both in similar ways don't we? We do drugs and eat unhealthy foods, we do not exercise properly or practice hygiene as we should, and we are not particularly attentive to imbalances when they occur. The same for all could be said concerning our interaction with Mother Earth.

We drill into her and cut into her with cruel abandon. We pluck and plunder her resources, her treasure and jewels, and suck the water from beneath her parched skin only to wonder why she buckles and convulses while reacting to the violation. Where everything once served a purpose now nothing makes any sense. We drill offshore and on land retrieving fossil fuels to run inefficient heating systems and operate antiquated engines. We divert water from ancient streams and rivers to irrigate new crops on old land that farmers are increasingly paid not to grow. We build and operate nuclear facilities

WHEN NO PLAN EXISTS TO DISPOSE OF THE WASTE. WE EXPLODE NUCLEAR WARHEADS DEEP INSIDE OUR MOTHER'S BELLY WITH NO REGARD TO CONSEQUENCE EVEN WHEN THE TECHNOLOGY IS PRESENT TO CONDUCT ALL TESTS WITH COMPUTER SIMULATION. WE CONTINUE TO LOG OLD GROWTH FORESTS TO SUPPLY BUILDING MATERIAL WHEN THE TECHNOLOGY IS PRESENT TO DEVELOP SYNTHETIC ALTERNATIVES. WE AS A SPECIES, CLEAR CUT MILLIONS OF ACRES IN THE RAIN FORESTS SO THAT BEEF CAN BE RAISED FOR MCDONALD'S, THEN WONDER WHY THE RAINWATER WHICH WAS ONCE PLENTIFUL, NOW HAS TO BE DRILLED FOR OR PUMPED IN FROM OUTSIDE SOURCES. WE STRIP MINE THE SKIN FROM OUR MOTHER LEAVING HER WITH FESTERING AND OPEN SORES.

IT IS DISGUSTINGLY IMMORAL AND IRRESPONSIBLE BEHAVIOR.

AIR:

THERE SHOULD BE ZERO TOLERANCE WHERE COMMERCIAL POLLUTION IS EVIDENT. THE TECHNOLOGY AND SYSTEMS ARE AVAILABLE NOW TO ACHIEVE PURE AIR QUALITY LEVELS IN EVERY INDUSTRY IN AMERICA. THERE SIMPLY IS NO INCENTIVE TO EMPLOY THEM.

NON COMPLIANCE BY THE PRIVATE SECTOR SHOULD BE DEALT WITH HARSHLY. A $100,000 DOLLAR FINE MEANS NOTHING TO A $20,000,000 COMPANY. WHEN THE FINES REACH EIGHT FIGURES, CHANGE WILL OCCUR.

THE FIRST AND MOST DIRECT OF THE INCENTIVES TO CLEAN UP CORPORATE EXHAUST WOULD BE BY DIRECT GOVERNMENT ORDER UNDER THREAT TO NATIONAL HEATH AND WELFARE. NON COMPLIANCE WITH THE ORDER WOULD CAUSE INTERVENTION (MILITARY IF NECESSARY) AND NATIONAL ACQUISITION OF OWNERSHIP.

THE SECOND INCENTIVE SHOULD BE STRUCTURED IN THE FORM OF A PACKAGE OF TAX BREAKS THAT WOULD PROVIDE PRORATED RELIEF OVER A NUMBER OF YEARS BUT WOULD NOT EXCUSE THE ENTIRE COST OF THE CLEAN UP.

The third incentive would be in the form of long term loans granted from both the private and public sectors much like bond measures but repaid by the businesses.

All the retrofitting necessary should be accomplished within ten years from the date of the directive at which time the commercial exhaust of America would be pollution free.

Internal combustion engines should be modified to operate on alternate fuel sources which are currently available within ten years. The good old boy contracts with carburetion companies and refineries would become immediately null and void by direct order of the government.

Emphasis on development for alternate fuels should be on compounds or mixtures other than natural gas.

Most climatologists feel that by the end of the twenty first century, Earth's surface temperature will have increased up to ten degrees as a result of the continued pollution by greenhouse gases and carbon dioxide.

Efficient mass transportation systems need to be built in all of our cities. The propulsion method should be hydrogen. Electrical energy appears attractive as an alternative to petroleum products but the emissions removed on the street side are replaced by those produced with the increased mining and drilling required to fuel the generators. The mass transit enterprise should be controlled by the private sector, no government intervention should be allowed save a one time subsidy if necessary.

Americans should be encouraged to use mass transit. That encouragement could come in the form of tax breaks for documented use or a deduction for not owning an automobile. There are a multitude of other creative incentives available that would discourage driving, any one of which or combination may be attractive to an individual depending on his/her needs.

The space exploration program should be required to retrieve the waste it has discarded on the moon and in the solar system where at all possible without creating an entire new industry of inter galactic garbage trucks. They should be prohibited in the future from leaving any debris behind regardless of the focus of project.

Energy:

The large oil refineries located within the borders of the United States of America should be required to close shop within fifteen years.

They would be allowed to sell their product in the U.S. for the ten years of the internal combustion engine's conversion to alternate fuels, and then allowed to sell beyond our borders for the remaining five. It would certainly behoove them if they took the initiative and reoriented their R&D divisions to alternate fuel development. Most likely, much of the same equipment could be used, although that is simply a common sense observation, anathema to a business community who has been burglarizing the public since the engines invention.

After fifteen years no more petroleum products will be removed from the Earth and Oceans of America. The refineries will continue to do business overseas much as the tobacco companies have, but their business will cease in the United States.

All nuclear power plants operating in America will be shut down in five years UNLESS a safe and permanent means of nuclear waste disposal is developed.

There exist a multitude of alternative energy options, most not pursued because the current method of operation is too convenient and profitable. Hydroelectric, geothermal, and solar are three accessible and clean

SOURCES OF ENERGY THAT HAVE EXPERIENCED ONLY LIMITED USE IN TERMS OF THE TOTAL DEMAND. WHAT'S HAPPENED TO HARNESSING THE WIND? ALL THAT WOULD BE REQUIRED IS TO HOOK UP FANS IN FRONT OF THE FACES OF ALL THE LOBBYISTS AND POLITICIANS. ALTERNATE FUELS THAT ARE NON POLLUTING AND INEXPENSIVE (AS WILL BE USED IN OUR CARS) PRESENT ANOTHER CHOICE.

THE FOCUS SHOULD BE ON ELIMINATING DEPENDENCY ON ANY KIND OF FUEL SOURCE THAT MUST PHYSICALLY BE REMOVED FROM EARTH SUCH AS PETROLEUM SOURCES INCLUDING NATURAL GASES.

COMPANIES THAT WISH TO ASSIST CONVERSION SHOULD BE PROVIDED WITH EVERY INCENTIVE TO DO SO.

FORESTS:

WITH THE EXCEPTION OF CONTROLLED BURNS AND NECESSARY THINNING, LOGGING SHOULD BE REDUCED TO 15% OF ITS CURRENT ACTIVITY IN FIVE YEARS. A FORTY YEAR MORATORIUM WOULD THEN BE IMPOSED HOLDING THE INDUSTRY TO THE 15% OPERATION LEVEL.

CURRENTLY, MORE THAN 35 MILLION ACRES OF FOREST ARE CUT OR BURNED EACH YEAR.

QUITE FRANKLY, WHENEVER I HEAR THE OFT QUOTED SAYING IN THE NORTHWEST, "NEXT TIME YOU RUN SHORT OF PAPER PRODUCTS, WIPE YOUR ASS WITH THE SPOTTED OWL", I CAN'T HELP BUT THINK THAT THERE ARE NOT ENOUGH SPOTTED OWLS ALIVE TO WIPE ALL THOSE ASSHOLES.

LUMBER COMPANIES WOULD BE ENCOURAGED WITH TAX INCENTIVES AND/OR LOANS TO DEVELOP WOOD RELATED COMPOUNDS THAT COULD BE USED TO REPLACE ALL WOOD PRODUCTS. THIS WOULD BE TEMPORARY IN TERMS OF RELIANCE ON WOOD FOR BUILDING AND PRINTING. THE ULTIMATE GOAL SHOULD BE TO INVENT AND DEVELOP SYNTHETIC SYSTEMS TO REPLACE THOSE DEPENDENT ON WOOD.

No more government BLM or Forest Service connected land will be sold to anyone, period. Accordingly, there will be no more mining hand outs under the old and archaic settlement law. It is estimated that America has given 200 billion dollars of land to big business for pennies because of a law that originally encouraged settlement of the country. Equitable land swaps for environmental reasons are appropriate but only under strict guidelines.

Snow mobiles will be restricted to areas where there is no ground cover and no endangered species located within twenty- five miles of the outer perimeter of the designated use zone. They will be required to use four stroke engines.

Three and four wheel all terrain utility vehicles will be restricted to existing paths and roads. If a hunter feels he is man enough to kill his prey, then he is man enough to carry that prey to his vehicle.

All areas that have been clear cut or logged will be replanted, the cost of which will be shared jointly by the government and the lumber companies.

Food providers would be aggressively encouraged to discover new recipes or ingredients that would reduce the demand for beef, as well as other meats, toward the ultimate goal of developing and serving food that does not require the slaughter of another living thing or deforestation of large areas of land for grazing.

All paper related industries would be encouraged by government directive to develop their recycling capability to a level where at this point in our history; it would represent the best effort possible.

All junk mail advertisers are going to have to sell their wares on the Internet, purchase TV time, or use some other electronic means to convey their message. Such advertising on paper and especially through the mail will be immediately prohibited.

Land:

All land that has become a victim of the callous exploitation of corporate interests needs to be cleaned up. Whether it is in Butte, Montana where strip mining is most evident or in the industrial drop zones of the big cities, aggressive action needs to be taken to begin the removal of toxins from the soil. The pollutants affect the air, the water, and the safety and well being of those living things that venture into or near the site.

The cost of the reclamation needs to born as much is ascertainable, by those who caused it, but with a caveat of fairness. Most of the information regarding hazardous waste has been recently discovered, in the last twenty to thirty years.

Hazardous waste could be synonymous in implication with a natural disaster. If studies of a particular site indicate that a danger is real and present, it would not be unreasonable to build one less missile or bomber and get it fixed. (See National Defense and Spending)

Tax breaks in combination with long term loans could be made available to companies occupying the polluted property.

Tax breaks and incentives should be made available to new businesses that specialize in toxic waste removal.

All gas driven leaf/lawn blowers would become illegal immediately.

Water:

The human animal's composition is over 90% water. Over 75% of planet Earth's surface is covered by water. Yet with both bodies we waste and pollute that which is most precious to us and essential to our survival.

David Hayden

There is a not often talked about problem common to every town and city in America. It has to do with the corrosion and disintegration of the pipes used to deliver fresh drinking water to our houses, offices, and all other facilities. The same can be said for the sewer systems in this country. The piping and pumps that were laid beneath our streets and alleys, and above ground, connecting our communities with both fresh water and waste disposal, are falling apart. New sewage treatment plants have to be designed that will not allow overflow or contamination during natural disasters such as flooding. The new plants should also be required to employ the latest in recyclable technology.

A co-coordinated effort between the public and private sector needs to be made to remove and replace both the old service lines and systems with new that will last at least another one hundred years. Much of this can be paid for once the tax system is overhauled thus eliminating the deficit and producing a surplus.

Compounding the problem, the current methods of collecting fresh water from rain and run off have become grossly inadequate given increased demand. Public works projects similar to those implemented during the depression have to be resurrected and applied throughout the land. Larger and stronger levees need to be built. Giant reservoirs need to be constructed in locations that will minimally impact the environment. Dams need to be built in environmentally suitable sites in the country. It is not unfeasible that a plan could be fashioned that could reduce the threat of flooding radically into the far future.

No more fresh water should be diverted from streams or rivers in America. Runoff and rain water collected in the new reservoirs can be used for agriculture and ranching. The ice runoff provides the water for the streams, rivers, and tributaries that have been supporting ecosystems long before man's interference. A classic case of runoff rip off exists at Pyramid Lake in Nevada.

The Piautes were guaranteed by the United States government that they alone owned the water feeding the ancient lake. Ranchers and farmers have siphoned off and diverted so much of the water that the level of the lake is at an all time low and falling fast. But then, the U.S. government broke close to 500 treaties with Native Americans; the faces change, the evil remains.

Close to a third of the world's human population has no access to healthy or safe water. Not much imagination is required to calculate the distress imposed on all of the other forms of life caused by our overpopulation and waste.

When a drought does occur as a consequence of poor water management on the behalf of our elected officials, restricted use should be imposed upon the major users, agriculture (especially those fields used for growing those crops that will never reach the market), and parks and recreation (golf courses both public and private). Residential water use accounts for less than 10% of consumption while agriculture accounts for over 70%, with the remainder used by big business and recreation.

The cry's, "Take short showers" and "don't flush" along with "don't water your yard" leap from the lips of the bureaucrats, once again unfairly expecting those citizens using or having the least to sacrifice the most, as it is with the current tax system. Until the water aspect changes, I say take long showers, water your yard, and flush as many times as you so desire. As an aside, please consider. We've always been told to only water in the morning or evening, when it's cooler outside. To my knowledge no one's ever bothered to question that drop of advice. The ground closes up (contracts) as the temperature falls. Water runs off the lawn rather than being absorbed. The run off falls into the gutter, then flows into a storm drain. In the heat of the day the ground expands and develops cracks much like a parched desert. The water is then absorbed into the open earth. The powers that be don't want any evaporation to occur because with their limited thought

THEY FEEL EVAPORATION IS A WASTE OF WATER. ACTUALLY EVAPORATION IS GOOD BECAUSE IT IS CONDUCIVE TO STIMULATING RAINFALL AND HUMIDITY, IN OTHER WORDS, GENERATING MORE WATER. THE WATER GOING DOWN THE STORM DRAIN IS WASTED.

JET SKI USE SHOULD BE RESTRICTED TO THOSE BODIES OF WATER THAT SUPPORT NO AQUATIC LIFE. TWO CYCLE ENGINES SHOULD BE PROHIBITED ON ANY BODY OF WATER.

THE OCEANS REMAIN OUR LAST TRUE FRONTIER. WE AS A SPECIES HAVE TOTALLY SCREWED UP ALL THE REST, WHY NOT LEAVE THIS ONE ALONE. AS IT IS WE'VE:

- WIPED OUT OR OVER FISHED CLOSE TO 70% OF ALL THE WORLD'S FISH STOCKS,
- VIRTUALLY DECIMATED THE WHALE POPULATION, ALL FOR THE SAKE OF OILS AND BLUBBER; AN ANIMAL WITH MORE INNATE INTELLIGENCE AND GRACE THAN WE COULD HOPE TO ACHIEVE IN LIFETIMES.
- BUILT GIANT OFFSHORE OIL RIGS THAT BY THEIR VERY NATURE ARE ENVIRONMENTAL ENEMIES; ALL TO RETRIEVE AN ANCIENT FUEL SOURCE TO USE IN INEFFICIENT MECHANICAL CONTRAPTIONS AND SYSTEMS. THE RIGS BY DESIGN CANNOT HELP BUT POLLUTE AT SOME POINT IN THE RECOVERY PROCESS.
- CONSTRUCTED TANKERS CAPABLE OF CARRYING MILLIONS OF GALLONS OF CRUDE OIL WHILE FAILING TO PROVIDE ANY METHOD OF CONTAINMENT WHEN OIL SPILLS OCCUR, OR WHILE FAILING TO BUILD THE SHIPS ADEQUATELY IN THE FIRST PLACE. IT SHOULD BE NO SURPRISE THAT THE ENORMOUS COST OF THE TANKERS IS ONE OF THE VERY LARGE REASONS NO ALTERNATIVE FUELS ARE BEING DEVELOPED.
- HAVE RAVISHED THE OCEANS WITH GARGANTUAN FLOATING FISH FACTORIES THAT INDISCRIMINATELY KILL EVERYTHING CAUGHT IN THEIR MILES LONG GILL NETS.
- HAVE DEVELOPED ALL THE TECHNOLOGY NECESSARY TO KILL AND MAKE EXTINCT ALL AQUATIC LIFE FORMS WITH NO PROVISION FOR REPLACEMENT.
- INVENTED INTRICATE SUBSURFACE MAPPING AND SEISMIC EQUIPMENT THAT EMPLOYS THE USE OF SONIC BOOMS WHICH STUN OR KILL ALL LIFE WITHIN ITS RANGE.

- ALLOW SHIPS TO DUMP THEIR WASTE OUTSIDE THE THREE MILE LIMIT AS IF CURRENTS AND MOTION DON'T EXIST. WE DO THIS WITH THE UNDERSTANDING THAT FISH LIKE EATING SHIT; THEN WE EAT THE FISH, THE SAME FISH WE'VE FED CRAP TO, LUBED WITH CRUDE, STUNNED OR DISABLED, AND TRAPPED IN CAGES AND NETS THEREBY ALTERING THEIR CENTRAL NERVOUS SYSTEMS TO THE EXTENT THAT THEIR CHEMICAL REACTION TO OUR ATTACKS TAINTS THEIR MEAT.
- AT TIMES OF SEWER PLANT OR SEWER LINE FAILURE, ALLOWING THE EFFLUENTS TO DISCHARGE INTO THE SEA. DISCHARGE IS INDEED THE OPERABLE WORD, IT IS CLINICALLY USED WHEN HUMANS SECRET FLUIDS FROM INFECTIONS. OUR COLLECTIVE FAILURE IS AN INFECTION, AND IT'S POLLUTING THE WORLD.

WE DO THESE CRUEL AND INHUMANE THINGS TO PROTECT OUR FUTURE WITHOUT CONSIDERING THAT ALL AROUND US, ABOVE US, AND BENEATH US, IS OUR FUTURE.

GOD

The most important question among all humans concerns the existence and form of God.

Mankind has been perplexed and puzzled by a Higher Power since cave dwelling.

Early man considered thunder and lightening to be Godlike or certainly instruments of God. Variations along that line of thought survived/evolved into Greek mythology where people believed Gods in human form ruled elements of the universe.

Others believe in Animism, Buddha, Jehovah, The Queen of the Heavens, Gods of the Four Corners, or totems and figurines.

Atheists deny the existence of God.

Those that can actually see the object of their adoration have an easier time with the belief aspect of their earthly statue's concomitant powers.

Spirituality is a very private and personal exercise.

All Christians rely mostly on faith. It is true that statues of Jesus populate places of worship the world over and adorn the mantels and walls of most homes, yet Jesus is one third of the Holy Trinity; Father, Son, and Holy Ghost.

Those individuals who believe solely in creation and gardens with Adam and Eve are certainly entitled to their opinion.

Those who believe solely in evolution are equally entitled.

If one states unequivocally, based on a book (Bible) and/or faith that God created the earth along with

ALL SPECIES OF PLANT AND ANIMAL LIFE, THAT BELIEF IS THEIR CONSTITUTIONAL RIGHT.

IF CONVERSELY, THE EVOLUTIONIST EMBRACES THE "BIG BANG" THEORY, THAT PERSON IS ALSO PROTECTED.

THE TRUTH IS THAT NO ONE KNOWS ANYTHING, FOR SURE!

THE QUESTIONS OF THE FUTURE ARE, "WHO CREATED OR HOW WAS GOD CREATED?", AND "WHO OR WHAT CAUSED THE BIG BANG?"

WHILE IT MIGHT BE INTELLECTUALLY INVIGORATING TO CONTEMPLATE SUCH COLOSSAL QUESTIONS, WE ARE NOT EQUIPPED TO COMPREHEND THE ANSWERS.

MY POINT IS THIS, WHY DOES EVERYTHING IN THE HUMAN WORLD HAVE TO BE ONE OR THE OTHER?

IT IS PREPOSTEROUS TO INSIST ON ONE IDEOLOGY OVER ANOTHER, AND IT IS SAD THAT WE DO SO. WE SHOULD BE GLAD THAT PEOPLE HAVE A FAITH OR EVEN CONSIDER A "HIGHER" OR ELEVATED PRESENCE TO EXIST.

I HAVE HAD THE GOOD FORTUNE TO HAVE WITNESSED MIRACLES AND BEEN IN THE COMPANY OF ANGELS. I HAVE ALSO EXPERIENCED THE UNDERWORLD OR "OTHER SIDE", TO USE THE VERNACULAR.

POSSESSING ALL KNOWLEDGE OR HAVING ALL THE ANSWERS TO QUESTIONS OF EVOLUTION OR CREATION HAS NEVER BEEN A PRIORITY WITH ME.

LIVING RESPONSIBLY AND KINDLY WITH THE KNOWLEDGE WE HAVE HAS BEEN MY GOAL.

EONS FROM NOW, IN TEMPLATES OF TIME FAR INTO THE FUTURE, WE MAY LEARN ALL THE ANSWERS, THAT IS IF WE HAVEN'T DESTROYED OUR SPECIES AND ALL WITHIN OUR GRASP BEFORE THEN.

THEN IS THE ANSWER; THEN AND ONLY THEN WILL WE KNOW.

I SAY LET US DISCIPLINE OURSELVES, LET US BEHAVE RIGHTEOUSLY AND RESPONSIBLY, LET US NOT BE SO ARROGANT AND STUBBORN CONCERNING MATTERS BEYOND OUR ABILITY TO UNDERSTAND, AND LET'S STICK AROUND FOR THE TRUTH.

GUN CONTROL

"WE'VE ALMOST COME FULL CIRCLE, FROM THE OLD WILD WEST DAYS WHERE YOU HAD TO PACK A GUN FOR PROTECTION, TO THE PERIOD IN BETWEEN WHERE WE ALL RELIED ON THE POLICE FOR THAT FUNCTION, TO THE PRESENT WHERE THE POLICE ARE OUT GUNNED AND OUT NUMBERED AND INCREASINGLY BEING FORCED TO DEFEND NOT ONLY THE PUBLIC, BUT THEMSELVES IN INNER CITY WAR ZONES"

AMERICA IS ARMED, PERIOD!

No AMOUNT OF LEGISLATION, CONFISCATION, MEDIATION, OR OBFUSCATION WILL ALTER THE FACT THAT PERSONAL FIREPOWER IS TO THE OVERWHELMING MAJORITY OF CITIZENS, ONE OF THE DEAREST AND MOST SACRED OF THEIR INALIENABLE RIGHTS AS GUARANTEED BY THE SECOND AMENDMENT TO THE CONSTITUTION OF THE UNITED STATES OF AMERICA.

THE CAPTAINS OF COLONIALISM HAD EVERY REASON TO BE CONCERNED ABOUT PERSONAL SAFETY. LAW ENFORCEMENT WAS TENUOUS AT BEST, THE INDIGENOUS SPECIES OF HUMAN WERE PISSED OFF AT THE UNINVITED WHITE MAN, EUROPEANS WANTED WHAT THEY THOUGHT THE SETTLERS HAD, AND A REVOLUTIONARY WAR APPEARED IMMINENT.

THE SECOND AMENDMENT WAS A THOUGHTFUL MOVE ON THE PART OF THOSE MILITARY MAVERICKS SO MANY YEARS AGO.

THE AVAILABLE WEAPONS TWO HUNDRED PLUS YEARS AGO WERE CRUDE PISTOLS, MUSKETS, AND CANNON. THE OCCUPATION OF AMERICA COULD NEVER HAVE BEEN ACCOMPLISHED HAD IT NOT BEEN FOR THE SUPERIOR WEAPONS USED IN THE EFFORT. TECHNOLOGYRESPONDEDTOTHEDEMANDMADEBYGEOMETRICALLY INCREASING NUMBERS OF EXPATRIATES EITHER RUNNING FROM THE OLD WORLD AND/OR CHASING A NEW DREAM.

AT NO POINT IN THE HISTORY OF THE UNITED STATES DID ANYONE WITH CLOUT CONSIDER THAT JUST MAYBE, THE NEED FOR

PERSONAL PROTECTION HAD WANED AND IT MIGHT BE WISE TO CURB THE PUBLIC'S CONSUMPTION OF HAND GUNS.

IN ALL FAIRNESS, NO ONE COULD HAVE EVER ANTICIPATED THE EXTENT TO WHICH THE TECHNICAL AND INDUSTRIAL REVOLUTIONS WOULD INFLUENCE THE WORLD WITH EFFICIENT, VARIED, AND INCREASINGLY DESTRUCTIVE WEAPONS.

WAKE UP ALL YOU ANTI GUN WHINERS. UNTIL HUMAN/ANIMAL NATURE CHANGES, UNTIL WE BEGIN USING SIGNIFICANTLY MORE THAN THREE PER CENT OF OUR BRAIN, AND UNTIL WE MAKE SOME SERIOUS PROGRESS REGARDING ESTABLISHING OPPORTUNITY AND FAIRNESS, WHILE PROVIDING TO ALL CITIZENS THE ESSENTIAL ELEMENTS OF A CIVILIZED SOCIETY, WE BETTER KEEP THE GUNS.

THERE IS NO DOUBT THAT WE NEED BETTER REGULATION AND INSPECTION OF THE BUSINESS. TOWARD THAT END, LEGISLATION SHOULD BE PASSED REQUIRING THE FOLLOWING.

GUN DEALERS SHOULD BE LICENSED BY THE FEDERAL, STATE, AND LOCAL GOVERNMENTS IN WHICH THEY INTEND TO CONDUCT BUSINESS. THE THREE LICENSES SHOULD BE POSTED OR STORED IN A COMMON, NATIONAL COMPUTER.

THE DEALERS MUST OPERATE OUT OF A COMMERCIAL BUILDING THAT MEETS ALL APPLICABLE BUILDING AND SAFETY CODES. THAT OFFICE OR BUILDING MUST HAVE A STATE OF THE ART SECURITY SYSTEM INCLUDING MULTIPLE CAMERAS, ALARMS CONNECTED DIRECTLY TO LOCAL POLICE ALONG WITH ADEQUATE BATTERY BACKUP IN CASE OF A POWER FAILURE, AND LOCKS ON ALL WEAPONS FOR SALE.

IF AN INDIVIDUAL IS CAUGHT SELLING WEAPONS OUT OF AN AUTOMOBILE, RV, CATALOGUE, OR RESIDENCE, HE/SHE WILL BE CHARGED WITH A FELONY AND ALL OF HIS WEAPONS AND ACCESSORIES WILL BE PERMANENTLY SEIZED.

NO DEALER WILL BE ALLOWED TO SELL ASSAULT WEAPONS PERIOD. THE ONLY MEMBERS OF SOCIETY THAT WILL HAVE ACCESS TO WEAPONS OF WAR WILL BE THE MILITARY AND LAW ENFORCEMENT. IF A PERSON IS APPREHENDED WITH AN ASSAULT

WEAPON, IT ALONG WITH ALL WEAPONS POSSESSED OR OWNED WILL BE PERMANENTLY SEIZED. THE INDIVIDUAL WILL BE CHARGED WITH A FELONY AND PROHIBITED FOR LIFE FROM PURCHASING ANOTHER GUN.

THERE SHOULD BE A FIFTEEN DAY MANDATORY WAITING PERIOD FOR THE PURCHASE OF ANY RIFLE OR HANDGUN ANYWHERE IN THE UNITED STATES. THE NATIONAL CLEARANCE COMPUTER SHOULD BE LINKED TO ALL INTERNATIONAL ALLIES, AND OF COURSE, TO ALL LAW ENFORCEMENT AGENCIES IN AMERICA.

NO PERSON WILL BE ALLOWED TO BUY A WEAPON WHO IS NOT A UNITED STATES CITIZEN. A PERSON WILL BE REQUIRED TO PURCHASE ANY FIREARM IN HIS STATE OF RESIDENCE.

CITIZENS CAN PURCHASE ANY RIFLE, SHOTGUN, OR SEMI-AUTOMATIC PISTOL WITH A SEVENTEEN SHOT CLIP OR LESS, PROVIDING THAT THEY ARE OVER TWENTY ONE YEARS OF AGE.

A PROSPECTIVE BUYER WILL HAVE TO SHOW PROOF THAT HE/SHE SUCCESSFULLY COMPLETED A WEAPONS SAFETY AND USE CLASS IN ADDITION TO PASSING A MARKSMANSHIP TEST ON AN APPROVED RANGE. IN LIEU OF THAT REQUIREMENT, MEMBERS OF THE ARMED FORCES WOULD HAVE TO PROVIDE A COPY OF THEIR DD 214.

REMOVING WEAPONS FROM LAW ABIDING CITIZENS WILL DO NOTHING BUT JEOPARDIZE THEIR SAFETY. AS STATED EARLIER, NO LONGER CAN WE AS THE PUBLIC EXPECT LOCAL LAW ENFORCEMENT TO PROVIDE AN ACCEPTABLE LEVEL OF PROTECTION FOR OURSELVES, FAMILIES, AND LOVED ONES. THE ACCELERATING COLLAPSE OF SOCIETY COMBINED WITH BUDGET CUTS ALL BUT INSIST THAT ONE ASSUME A LARGER ROLE IN TERMS OF HIS/HER PERSONAL SAFETY. WE'VE ALMOST COME FULL CIRCLE, FROM THE OLD WILD WEST DAYS WHERE YOU HAD TO PACK A GUN FOR PROTECTION, TO THE PERIOD IN BETWEEN WHERE WE ALL RELIED ON THE POLICE FOR THAT FUNCTION, TO THE PRESENT WHERE THE POLICE ARE OUT GUNNED AND OUT NUMBERED AND INCREASINGLY BEING FORCED TO DEFEND NOT ONLY THE PUBLIC, BUT THEMSELVES IN INNER CITY WAR ZONES.

DAVID HAYDEN

PEOPLE QUITE SIMPLY ARE GOING TO HAVE TO ACCEPT THE FACT THAT THE BAD GUYS ARE ALWAYS GOING TO GET THEIR GUNS, THAT WE CAN MAKE CERTAIN THAT THEY FORCED TO DO THAT ILLEGALLY BY ADOPTING THE ABOVE STATED RULES FOR SALE, AND THAT UNLESS WE APPROPRIATE LARGE AMOUNTS OF MONEY FOR MORE POLICE AND BETTER TRAINING, WE HAD BETTER BE PREPARED TO "BITE THE BULLET" AND ASSUME RESPONSIBILITY FOR OUR OWN PROTECTION.

Health Care

"Assisted suicide should be legal and part of the package offered to the public. We had no conscious choice getting here, the least we can do is afford ourselves some degree of self determination on our way out"

There is no excuse whatsoever for not having a national health care policy that provides for all the citizens of the United States regardless of ethnicity or social standing. The only reason we don't is because the lobbyists for the AMA, pharmaceutical companies, HMO's, and insurance companies keep preventing Congress from enacting the necessary legislation.

It's more than ironic that these same purveyors of painlessness enjoy the very health care that they fight so hard to deny the general public.

Strictly from a financial perspective, many studies have already concluded that a comprehensive national health care system would cost less in the long run than we are currently spending through welfare, SSI, Medicare, and emergency treatment. Preventative medicine has always cost less than rehabilitation or surgery. People simply need access to the information.

As an example, proper pre natal care can usually prevent disease, disability, and/or deformity in an infant, three infinitely more expensive and perhaps unnecessary conditions had counseling and pre natal care been available.

If all people in America would FEEL that we exist as just small parts of the big whole; that recognition would truly serve to prove the truth of the old axiom that "A chain is only as strong as it's weakest link". One couldn't escape the symbiotic bonds of society if they had to, therefore it is in each person's best interest to make available to all

OTHERS THAT WHICH THEY SO DESIRE, AT LEAST IN TERMS OF THE BIG FIVE (HOUSING, CLOTHING, EDUCATION, HEALTH CARE, AND FOOD).

HEALTH CARE SHOULD BE MANDATORY AMONG EMPLOYERS REGARDLESS OF COMPANY SIZE. ALL EMPLOYEES SHOULD BE INCLUDED IN THE PROGRAM WHETHER THEY ARE FULL OR PART TIME. THE COMPANY SHOULD BE ABLE TO WRITE OFF UP TO FIFTY PER CENT OF THE COST ON THEIR TAXES.

ALL OTHER PEOPLE SHOULD BE ABLE TO ENTER ANY HEALTH CARE FACILITY AND BE TREATED. THE ONLY FORM OF IDENTIFICATION REQUIRED WOULD BE PROOF OF UNITED STATES CITIZENSHIP. CHARGES WOULD BE BILLED DIRECTLY TO THE NEW HEATH CARE AGENCY FOR PAYMENT. THE CHARGES WOULD BE BASED ON A SCALE OF NATIONAL AVERAGES TAKEN FROM EVERY HOSPITAL IN EVERY LARGE CITY IN THE UNITED STATES. SANCTIONS WOULD BE SEVERE FOR ANY HOSPITAL OR HEALTH CARE ORGANIZATION THAT DENIED TREATMENT TO ANY CITIZEN OR PADDED THE INVOICE.

HMO'S AND HOSPITALS WOULD BE REGULATED UNDER THREAT OF EXTREME FINES REGARDING THE RELATIONSHIP BETWEEN COST OF SERVICE AND CHARGE FOR SAME. FOR INSTANCE, HOSPITALS WILL ONLY BE ALLOWED TO CHARGE A REASONABLE MARK UP ON ALL OF ITS SERVICE ITEMS SUCH AS TOOTH BRUSHES, GOWNS, MEALS, SOAP, ETC. THERE IS NOTHING THAT WILL CONVINCE ME THAT A HOSPITAL TOOTHBRUSH SHOULD COST FIVE OR SIX BUCKS WHEN ONE CAN BE PURCHASED AT A CORNER PHARMACY FOR A FRACTION OF THAT PRICE.

THE NEW PUBLIC HEALTH CARE AGENCY SHOULD BE ADMINISTERED PRIVATELY, BY A FIRM LARGE ENOUGH TO HANDLE THE LOAD, AND BY ONE WITH NO POLITICAL TIES. REMEMBER, LOBBYING IS A FELONY. FOR THE SAKE OF CONTINUITY, THE CONTRACT AWARDED THE PRIVATE COMPANY SHOULD BE TEN YEARS IN LENGTH. AT THE EXPIRATION OF THE CONTRACT, NEW COMPANIES WOULD BE INVITED TO BID FOR THE WORK AND ENCOURAGED TO SHOWCASE NEW TECHNOLOGY WHICH WOULD SIMPLIFY AND EXPEDITE THE ACCOUNTING ASPECTS OF THE AGENCY. IT IS CONCEIVABLE THAT WITHIN A GENERATION COMPUTERS WILL HANDLE ALL BILLING AND PAYMENT PROCEDURES INDEPENDENT

OF A PERSON. THE EVENTUAL INEVITABILITY OF THAT HAPPENING IS UNSETTLING. THAT IS WHY IN SO MANY ARENAS OF LIFE IN AMERICA WE HAVE TO MAKE SOME ACCOMMODATION FOR INCREASINGLY LARGE NUMBERS OF PEOPLE WHO SIMPLY WILL NOT FIT INTO THE MAINSTREAM OF SOCIETY YET WILL STILL REQUIRE THE BASIC AMENITIES.

AMBULANCE COMPANIES NEED TO BE TIGHTLY SCRUTINIZED AND/OR REGULATED RELATIVE TO THEIR EXCESSIVE FEES. THE PARAMEDICS SHOULD BE PAID MORE.

TEENAGE GIRLS THAT GET PREGNANT NEED TO HAVE ACCESS TO IMMEDIATE COUNSELING, PRE NATAL INFORMATION, AND/ OR ABORTION. THEY DO NOT NEED THE PARENTS CONSENT. IF THE CONDITION (PREGNANCY) EXISTS, THAN THE PARENTS HAVE PROBABLY FAILED, AND WITH THE EXCEPTION OF FAMILIAL SUPPORT SHOULD ONLY HELP IN CONCERT WITH HEALTH CARE PROFESSIONALS TENDING TO WHAT HAS BECOME A SOCIAL CONCERN. BOTH THE TEENAGE FATHER AND MOTHER AND THEIR FOLKS SHOULD HAVE TO TAKE A SEX EDUCATION AND PARENTING COURSE. IF EITHER YOUNGSTER CAUSES ANOTHER TO OR BECOMES PREGNANT WHILE STILL A MINOR, THEY WILL BE STERILIZED.

IT WILL BE THE NEW AGENCIES FUNCTION TO MAKE CERTAIN THAT ALL THE PROGRAMS AND FACILITIES ARE AVAILABLE IN EVERY MAJOR CITY TO ADDRESS ALL THE MISCUES OF THE HUMAN ANIMAL. WE WILL NEED THE DRUG AND ALCOHOL CLINICS UP AND RUNNING, ABORTION CLINICS SAFE AND ACCESSIBLE, EMERGENCY ROOMS CLEAN AND WELL STAFFED, AND INFORMATION ABOUT ALL CIRCULATED IN PRIMARY GATHERING PLACES IN THE VARIOUS COMMUNITIES.

AIDS RESEARCH AND PREVENTION SHOULD SHARE THE NUMBER ONE PRIORITY WITH REPRODUCTION. THE GOVERNMENT SHOULD CUT THROUGH THE RED TAPE AND ATTACK AIDS AS IF IT WERE WW3, TO DO ANY LESS BORDERS ON THE CRIMINAL.

ASSISTED SUICIDE SHOULD BE LEGAL AND PART OF THE PACKAGE OFFERED TO THE PUBLIC. WE HAD NO CONSCIOUS CHOICE GETTING HERE; THE LEAST WE CAN DO IS AFFORD OURSELVES SOME DEGREE OF SELF DETERMINATION ON OUR WAY OUT.

NO ANIMALS SHOULD BE USED EXPERIMENTALLY IN LABORATORIES ANYWHERE FOR DRUG OR DISEASE RESEARCH. IT MAKES NO SENSE AT ALL TO VICTIMIZE DEFENSELESS ANIMALS FOR THE SOLE PURPOSE OF PROLONGING THE LIFE OF THE ONLY SPECIES THAT IS DESTROYING THE REST.

AND WHILE WE ARE AT IT, IT WOULDN'T BE A BAD IDEA TO TRY TO DEVELOP A TEST THAT COULD IDENTIFY AT BIRTH A SOCIOPATH, AND THEN BEGIN RESEARCH TO COME UP WITH A CURE. FOR EXAMPLE; IF THE GENE COULD BE IDENTIFIED THAT CONTROLS A CONSCIENCE (SUPEREGO) IT MIGHT BE POSSIBLE TO SURGICALLY ADD THAT INFLUENCE TO A BODY. THAT KIND OF FOCUS IS MUCH MORE IMPORTANT THAN CLONING AN IMPERFECT SPECIES.

HOMELESSNESS

"OUR NATION'S "LE MISERABLE" WILL OCCUPY THE
CONTINUALLY SPREADING BOTTOM OF THE SOCIAL PYRAMID,
STRUGGLING TO STAY ALIVE WHILE WAITING TO DIE"

HISTORICALLY, THE ISSUE OF HOMELESSNESS IS NOTHING NEW.

ALL CIVILIZATIONS, COUNTRIES, AND CULTURES HAVE HAD WITHIN THEIR CONFINES A PERCENTAGE OF POPULATION THAT, FOR A VARIETY OF REASONS, NEVER GAINED ACCESS TO THE MAINSTREAM OF SOCIETY. PEOPLE HAVE REACTED TO THAT CONDITION OR CIRCUMSTANCE IN AS MANY DIFFERENT WAYS AS WERE THEIR NUMBER, MANY UNFORTUNATELY HAVING NO CHOICE BUT TO LIVE IN THE STREETS.

IN MODERN TIMES, THERE HAS NEVER BEEN A COUNTRY AS PROSPEROUS AND PLENTIFUL AS AMERICA. THERE HAS ALSO NEVER BEEN A COUNTRY AS DRIVEN BY A DREAM, OR ONE AS WELL EQUIPPED STRUCTURALLY AND SPIRITUALLY TO ASSIST THOSE LESS FORTUNATE.

IT IS TRAGIC THAT THE TWO CONDITIONS MOST OFTEN CONFLICT, MADE MORE SO BECAUSE THIS COUNTRIES FAILURE TO UNITE IT'S RESOURCES IS CAUSED BY A SIMPLE SKIP IN PERCEPTION, RATHER THAN BY SOME QUANTUM LEAP IN LOGIC. IT ALL GOES BACK ONCE AGAIN TO THE QUESTION WHETHER OR NOT THE COLLECTIVE WELL BEING WOULD BE AUTOMATICALLY IMPROVED WITH THE INVOLVEMENT OF JUST ANOTHER PERCENT OR SO OF THE BRAIN RESULTING OF COURSE IN HIGHER IQ'S. REGARDLESS, IT IS CLEAR THAT WHAT'S GOING ON ISN'T WORKING AND THAT THE SITUATION IS RAPIDLY GETTING WORSE.

IT IS A SAD AND SORROWFUL FACT THAT ONLY SEVENTEEN PERCENT OF ALL PEOPLE ON THE PLANET ARE BORN INTO AN ENVIRONMENT CONDUCIVE TO FREEDOM AND SELF DETERMINATION, AND OF THE SEVENTEEN PERCENT, LESS THAN TEN PERCENT HAVE ACCESS TO THE TOOLS NECESSARY TO ACHIEVE JUST A CHANCE

FOR A FAIR SHOT AT THE COMFORT AND SECURITY THE OTHER SEVEN PERCENT TAKE FOR GRANTED.

GLOBALLY, ONE QUARTER OF THE PEOPLE LIVE ON LESS THAN ONE DOLLAR A DAY.

ON ANY GIVEN NIGHT IN AMERICA, CLOSE TO ONE MILLION PEOPLE ARE HOMELESS.

EIGHTEEN PER CENT OF THE PEOPLE IN AMERICA OWN ALL THE PROPERTY, MEANING THAT EIGHTY TWO PER CENT ARE RENTING OR ARE HOMELESS. I'VE NEVER HEARD A BETTER ARGUMENT FOR LANDLORD/TENANT REFORM.

LAND OWNERSHIP AND RENTAL IS NOTHING MORE THAN A CONTINUATION OF THE FEUDAL RELATIONSHIP BETWEEN SERFS AND LORDS. STRICT CODES OF RESPONSIBILITY NEED TO BE WRITTEN AND ENFORCED THAT APPLY TO LANDLORDS INVOLVING NOT ONLY SAFETY AND HEALTH ISSUES, BUT ALSO INCLUDING AESTHETIC CONSIDERATIONS SUCH AS LANDSCAPING, AND PAINT, AS EXAMPLES.

TENANTS SHOULD BE PROTECTED FROM THE WHIM OF THE PROPERTY OWNER WITH A NEW CODE OF RIGHTS THAT AFFORD RENTERS GREATER LATITUDE IN OCCASIONS OF EVICTIONS CAUSED BY SALE OR UNFORESEEN CATASTROPHE. ADDITIONALLY, DEPOSITS NEED TO BE REDUCED TO FAIR AMOUNTS WHICH IN TURN SHOULD BE REFUNDED WITH INTEREST AT EXPIRATION OF THE TENANCY. THE BURDEN OF PROOF REGARDING PROPERTY DAMAGE MUST REST WITH THE OWNER AND NOT THE TENANT.

THEREALTRUTHISTHATTHISEPIDEMICOFDISENFRANCHISEMENT AND EXCLUSION HAS REAL CAUSES, CAN BE UNDERSTOOD, AND COULD, WITH SOME SACRIFICE AND REORGANIZATION, BE COMPASSIONATELY CORRECTED IF THE COLLECTIVE CONSCIENCE OF A NATION SO DESIRES.

SOLVING THE "PROBLEM" IS SIMPLY A MATTER OF PRIORITY; ALWAYS HAS BEEN.

Choices have to be made between jails and schools, more shelters or more mansions, more highways or more mass transit, national health care for all or continued horror with the HMO's, clothing for all or full closets for a few, and while it seemed for a while that we as a society could ignore the problem largely because it didn't exist on our property, we find ourselves tripping over, smelling, and trying to avoid the stares of the victims of a failed system.

It is a portrait painted on the face of America. It is the classic struggle between the normal (whatever that is) and the abnormal, the assimilated and those who aren't, the have's and have not's, the abandoned veterans and the country who wishes they'd just go away, along with a whole new generation of people who have no hope or future in a country that seems to have forgotten them.

When a person is permanently denied access to all the promised stuff, he/she becomes a problem. Those bipedal problems staking out and stalking the streets are the fastest growing group of folks in the United States.

Without immediate and drastic revision of our approach to helping the homeless, the situation will reach critical mass and melt down within the next couple of decades. The relatively small yet distinct class of people that comprise the homeless will be joined in whole or part by the next two generations of Americans. They will be born into poverty, perhaps have one parent, will have no opportunity for education, food, housing, or medical care. Our nation's "Le Miserable" will occupy the continually spreading bottom of the social pyramid struggling to stay alive while waiting to die.

The projects we already have in the inner cities will look like palaces when compared to their future counterparts. Looking beyond the first person and the greed, a government that controls all the natural resources, has world supremacy in technical and industrial capability, and continues to claim superiority in

ALL THINGS SECULAR, HAS AN OBLIGATION AND A DUTY TO PROVIDE FOR ALL LIVING THINGS WITHIN ITS BORDERS.

THAT DUTY IS TO SUBTLY ADVANCE THE CAUSE OF SPIRITUAL AND METAPHYSICAL EVOLUTION BY PROVIDING AT LEAST THE MINIMUM IN TERMS OF SAFETY AND CARE TO ALL OF ITS CITIZENS. TO DENY THAT DUTY IS TO INVITE CULTURAL DESPAIR AND SOCIAL DECOMPOSITION.

PARAPHRASING THE FRENCH PHILOSOPHER ROUSSEAU, "PEOPLE DO HAVE THE RESPONSIBILITY TO HELP THOSE LESS FORTUNATE."

AN ADDED ADVANTAGE IN OUR OVER POPULATED AND "MODERN" WORLD IS THAT IN HELPING OTHERS WE WILL TRAVEL FAR TOWARD GUARANTEEING FUTURE GENERATIONS A SAFE AND SECURE WORLD AT BEST, OR POSTPONING THE INEVITABLE AT WORST. IT IS SOCIALLY SELF DESTRUCTIVE TO DENY A COUNTRY'S CITIZENRY THE MEANS NECESSARY FOR SELF IMPROVEMENT.

MOST OF THE REQUIRED MECHANISMS ARE ESSENTIALLY ALREADY IN PLACE TO HELP THE HOMELESS. THE PRIMARY OBSTACLE/ PROBLEM IN ANY CITY HAS ALWAYS BEEN THE BUREAUCRATIC BULLSHIT AND RELUCTANCE OF ELECTED ASSHOLES TO OFFEND THE CONSTITUENTS THEY COUNT ON FOR CAMPAIGN CONTRIBUTIONS.

HERE'S WHAT SHOULD HAPPEN.

HIRE A GROUP OF COLLEGE STUDENTS WITH SOCIAL SCIENCE MAJORS TO CONDUCT A ONE MONTH STUDY THROUGHOUT THE CITY TO DETERMINE AS CAN BEST BE THROUGH OBSERVATION, THE NUMBERS AND LOCATION OF THE HOMELESS POPULATION BASED ON ETHNICITY, GENDER, APPROXIMATE AGE, MOBILITY, AND EFFORT. BY EFFORT I MEAN TO WHAT EXTENT THE HOMELESS INDIVIDUAL ATTEMPTS TO SECURE MONEY OR FOOD, I.E., DO THEY HOLD A SIGN AT INTERSECTIONS ALL DAY OR DO THEY HANG OUT IN ALLEYS GOING THROUGH GARBAGE CONTAINERS. MOST IMPORTANTLY, WHERE ARE THE CHILDREN, IF ANY.

CONDUCT A TITLE SEARCH OF ALL UNOCCUPIED COMMERCIAL PROPERTY (PREFERABLY IN LIGHT INDUSTRIAL AREAS) THAT ARE

IN TAX DEFAULT OR HAVE BEEN SEIZED IN CONJUNCTION WITH A CRIMINAL CASE.

ALL THE APPROPRIATE INSPECTORS SHOULD BE SENT IN TO DETERMINE POTENTIAL HABITABILITY.

THE CITY OR COUNTY SHOULD THEN CLAIM THE PROPERTIES, DEED SAID REAL ESTATE TO ITSELF (THEY NEVER HAVE A PROBLEM WITH EMINENT DOMAIN) WHICH WOULD PROVIDE IMMEDIATE EQUITY AND ELIMINATE ANY SECOND OR THIRD PARTY INTERFERENCE, AND DECLARE THE BUILDINGS TAX FREE ZONES.

AT THIS POINT A TYPE OF SOCIAL TRIAGE WOULD HAVE TO OCCUR TO ADEQUATELY, SAFELY, AND FAIRLY ASSIST THE HOMELESS ACCORDING TO THEIR SEPARATE NEEDS.

FOR INSTANCE, ONE BUILDING OR SHELTER WOULD BE DESIGNED TO ACCOMMODATE FOLKS THAT ARE CAPABLE OF WORK AND INDEPENDENT LIVING BUT HAD "FALLEN ON HARD TIMES', BEEN THE VICTIM OF "DOWNSIZING", OR A VICTIM OF A NATURAL CATASTROPHE.

THEIR STAY IN THE SHELTER WOULD BE SHORT TERM. UPON ARRIVAL THEY WOULD BATHE, RECEIVE CLEAN CLOTHES, A COMPLETE PHYSICAL EXAMINATION, NUTRITIOUS MEALS, APPROPRIATE COUNSELING AND/OR THERAPY IF DRUG OR ALCOHOL DEPENDENT, RESIDENTIAL AND VOCATIONAL PLACEMENT OR ASSISTANCE, AND FINANCIAL HELP WHETHER IT BE IN THE FORM OF HUD, FOOD STAMPS, ATD, SOCIAL SECURITY, ETC., AS THEY EXIT THE SHELTER EN ROUTE TO A SECOND OR NEXT CHANCE.

EMPHASIS WOULD BE MADE TO KEEP THE FAMILY UNIT TOGETHER IF AT ALL POSSIBLE. HOWEVER, IF THE PARENTS ARE UNFIT FOR OBVIOUS REASONS THE CHILD OR CHILDREN WILL BE PLACED IN A NURTURING ENVIRONMENT. IF THE MOTHER OR FATHER HAS HAD MORE THAN TWO CHILDREN, THEY WILL BE STERILIZED.

THE SECOND TYPE OF FACILITY WOULD BE FOR THOSE LONG TERM HOMELESS THAT ARE INCAPABLE OF SELF SUPPORT OR EVEN PROVIDING THEMSELVES WITH THE BASICS SUCH AS SUSTENANCE, HYGIENE, AND SHELTER. THESE FOLKS COULD BE THE VICTIMS

OF THE REAGAN ERA IN CALIFORNIA (FOR EXAMPLE) WHEN RONNIE SUMMARILY SHUT DOWN MOST OF THE MENTAL HEALTH INSTITUTIONS. MANY OF HIS VICTIMS AND OTHERS ARE OFTEN SERIOUSLY MENTALLY ILL, PHYSICALLY CHALLENGED, OR VETERANS SO WOUNDED FROM THE WAR THAT THEY ARE HELD HOSTAGE BY THE HORROR AND FROZEN BY THE FIRE.

THESE CITIZENS WOULD EXPERIENCE THE SAME SCREENING AS THE FIRST GROUP BUT WOULD BE DENIED RE-ENTRY INTO SOCIETY UNTIL THEY'D SUCCESSFULLY COMPLETED ALL THE REQUIRED THERAPY AND COUNSELING THAT COMPETENT MEDICAL HEALTH PROFESSIONALS DEEMED NECESSARY. THE BUILDING THAT THIS SECOND GROUP WOULD BE HOUSED IN COULD BE COMPARED TO A JAIL IN THAT THEY WOULD NOT BE ALLOWED TO LEAVE. WITHIN THE WALLS AND HALLS HOWEVER, ALL WOULD ENJOY FREEDOM TO DO WHATEVER THEY WISHED AS LONG AS IT DIDN'T PRESENT A DANGER TO ANOTHER.

ANY CHILDREN FOUND IN THE CUSTODY OF THE SECOND GROUP WILL BE PERMANENTLY PLACED IN A HEALTHY AND MORE PROMISING ENVIRONMENT. THE PARENT(S) WILL BE PERMANENTLY STERILIZED.

EVERY EFFORT WOULD BE MADE TO FIND RELATIVES OF BOTH GROUPS.

THE THIRD GROUP WOULD PROBABLY END UP IN JAIL. THESE FOLKS WOULD BE VIOLENT, NON CO-OPERATIVE, AND PRESENT A DANGER TO THE STAFF AND OTHER OCCUPANTS.

BASED ON THE SPECIFIC STRUCTURAL REQUIREMENTS FOR GROUP ONE OR TWO, PLANS WOULD BE DRAWN TO BEGIN THE BUILDING PROCESS.

A PROJECT MANAGER SHOULD BE HIRED FROM THE PRIVATE SECTOR TO OVERSEE THE REQUIRED REMODELING AND RETROFITTING.

ALL PERMITS AND INSPECTIONS SHOULD BE EXPEDITED AND IMMUNE FROM RED TAPE OR POLITICAL POSTURING. ANY POLITICIAN

OR DESK JOCKEY WHO IMPEDES PROGRESS SHOULD BE REMOVED FROM OFFICE.

MOST IF NOT ALL OF THE LABOR NECESSARY TO DO THE WORK SHOULD COME FROM TRADES EXPERIENCED MINIMUM SECURITY INMATES, WELFARE RECIPIENTS, AND FINED OR TAX DELINQUENT GENERAL CONTRACTORS.

THE NECESSARY MATERIAL SHOULD COME FROM GOVERNMENT SURPLUSES, INVENTORIES OF SEIZED OR ASSUMED PROPERTIES OR BUILDING SUPPLY OUTLETS THAT HAVE OUTSTANDING TAX LIABILITY AND/OR FINES.

WITH THE EXCEPTION OF THE THIRD GROUP OF INDIVIDUALS, LAW ENFORCEMENT INVOLVEMENT IN THE HOMELESS PROBLEM WOULD BE DRAMATICALLY REDUCED, WITH CLEAR BENEFITS TO THE PUBLIC. AS AN EXAMPLE, SAN FRANCISCO SPENDS OVER FORTY MILLION DOLLARS ANNUALLY JUST DEALING WITH THE SITUATION. MOST OF THE MONEY IS SPENT PICKING PEOPLE UP AND INCARCERATING THEM FOR ONE NIGHT BEFORE THEY ARE BACK ON THE STREETS. THE HOMELESS RECEIVE NO HELP, THE COPS HAVE MORE SERIOUS THINGS TO DO IN TERMS OF PUBLIC SAFETY, AND UNLESS CHANGES ARE MADE, THE FINANCIAL AND HUMAN COST WILL CONTINUE TO ESCALATE.

WHEN THE BUILDINGS ARE CLEARED FOR OCCUPANCY AND STAFFED, VANS MANNED BY RESERVE POLICE WILL CRUISE THE STREETS, PARKS, AND ALLEYS, PICKING UP THE HOMELESS AND TRANSPORTING THEM TO THE APPROPRIATE SHELTER.

THE HOMELESS WILL HAVE NO CHOICE BUT TO GO. IF THEY RESIST, THE POLICE WILL ASSIST, PERIOD. LIVING ON THE STREETS WILL NO LONGER BE AN OPTION. IT IS A TRAGEDY OF ENORMOUS PROPORTIONS THAT SUCH A SITUATION DEVELOPED.

JUST AS A PERSON HAS THE RIGHT TO LIVE THEIR LIFE IN ANY SOCIALLY ACCEPTABLE MANNER THEY CHOOSE, SO HAS SOCIETY THE RIGHT NOT TO BE ACCOSTED, TO HAVE TO DETOUR AROUND SLEEPING OR SITTING PEOPLE, FECES, URINE, OR GENERALLY BE VISUALLY OR AUDIBLY EXPOSED TO THE POLLUTION OF POVERTY IN THE EXTREME.

I AM NOT ENCOURAGING GESTAPO TACTICS, OR POLICE STATES, OR DENIAL OF CIVIL RIGHTS.

THE RIGHTS OF A FEW, (MOST OF WHOM ARE NOT EVEN AWARE THAT THEY ARE DOING IT), TO LIVE IN A BASE, FILTHY, AND INFECTED FASHION DOES NOT SUPERSEDE THE RIGHTS OF THE MANY WHO DAILY GO TO GREAT LENGTHS REGARDLESS OF THEIR SOCIAL CIRCUMSTANCE TO AT LEAST INJECT SOME SEMBLANCE OF DIGNITY IN THEIR LIVES. I AM SUGGESTING AN ECONOMICAL AND COMPASSIONATE PROCESS THAT WILL BENEFIT BOTH SOCIETY AND THOSE UNFORTUNATE BEINGS, WHO OFTEN THROUGH NO FAULT OF THEIR OWN FOUND THEMSELVES ON THE DARK SIDE OF THE DREAM WITH NO FLASHLIGHT.

IMMIGRATION

"ALL OF THE PROBLEMS THAT PEOPLE HAVE WITH EACH
OTHER INTERNATIONALLY WILL THRIVE WITH FAR MORE
EXTREME CONSEQUENCES; ALL IN THE SAME COUNTRY THAT
THREE HUNDRED YEARS EARLIER OFFERED EVERYTHING,
AND IN SO DOING, ENDED UP WITH NOTHING"

IMMIGRATION HAS BEEN AN INTEGRAL PART OF HUMAN/ANIMAL
BEHAVIOR SINCE WE WERE CAVE DWELLERS. PEOPLE MOVED
FROM CAVE TO CAVE, COUNTRY TO COUNTRY, AND CONTINENT TO
CONTINENT PILLAGING AND PLUNDERING ALL THINGS IN THEIR
PATHS. LIKE LOCUSTS THEY ARE SWARMING OUR MOTHER EARTH
DEVOURING AND DESTROYING ALL OTHER LIVING THINGS. NORTH
AMERICA WAS CERTAINLY NO EXCEPTION. WE HAVE ONLY TRADED
OUR CAVES FOR CONDOS.

POLITICAL EXILES, EXPATRIATES, AND CRIMINALS COLONIZED
THE EAST COAST OF THIS COUNTRY BY INTRODUCING DISEASE AND
GENOCIDE TO THE NATIVE AMERICAN INDIANS (NAMED INDIANS BY
COLUMBUS AND OTHERS WHO CONSIDERED THEM ABORIGINALS
WHILE THINKING THAT THEY HAD LANDED IN THE INDIES), IMPORTING
AFRICAN AMERICANS AS SLAVES (WHO HAD BEEN PURCHASED
FROM THEIR OWN PEOPLE), IMPORTING CHINESE AS INDENTURED
SERVANTS, AND REMOVING THE MEXICANS FROM THE SOUTHWEST
WHICH HAD BEEN THEIR HOME FOR HUNDREDS OF YEARS.

THE FOUNDING FATHERS COLLECTIVELY CAME TO AMERICA
WITH THEIR WEAPONS AND THEIR GREED INTENT ON CONTROLLING
OR ELIMINATING ANY OTHER PEOPLE OR OBSTACLE IN THEIR PATH.

THEIR POLICIES OF EXPLOITATION WERE REWARDED WITH
MUCH SUCCESS. TO ENSURE IT CONTINUED, THE ENSLAVERS
WROTE THE DECLARATION OF INDEPENDENCE THEN DRAFTED THE
CONSTITUTION OF THE UNITED STATES OF AMERICA; VILLAINOUS
VISIONARIES ALL. WHO BETTER THOUGH TO CREATE A DOCUMENT
ESPOUSING FREEDOM WITH FEW RESTRICTIONS THAN A COLLECTION
OF CROOKS?

Most of the framers of Constitution owned slaves. None of them died poor. One does not have to possess a Ph.D. in perception to understand the dynamic.

The new Americans got a lot done in historically a very short period of time.

Globally, humans numbered less than five hundred million two hundred and fifty years ago. The population is close to two hundred and eighty million today in the United States alone. The world population is closing in on seven billion thanks in large part to irresponsible coupling.

Dreams can easily become nightmares as we all know. Tough decisions have to be made regarding immigration in the twenty first century. If ideally, the citizens of the United States lived in a society free from racism, sexism, hatred, and violence, discussions of any of these issues would be unnecessary. The irony in the whole deal is that the image or model of America in most minds' remains true to the stated goals penned in historic charters, which is that this country evolved from the rubble of anarchy and revolution thereby setting a standard of achievement, fairness, and freedom for the rest of the world.

The truth is that America is in turmoil. Its social infrastructure is in an accelerating state of collapse. Paranoia, anger, resentment, and corporate exploitation are the rule not the exception. No provision exists for the people that live here <u>now</u>, who will never participate in society, who will never find work, live in a permanent home, be adequately fed, have access to health care, and are destined to forever remain prisoners of a system poisoned by selfishness and greed.

What are we going to do (speaking in a global context)? Are we all going to sink together, or are we going to swim together? To avoid sinking, radical changes have to be made that will initially seem inhumane and unfair. Do we still allow one million plus immigrants into America

ANNUALLY EVEN THOUGH MOST OF THEM DON'T SPEAK ENGLISH, HAVE NO FINANCIAL RESOURCES, NO REPRODUCTIVE RESTRAINT, AND FEW MARKETABLE SKILLS.

IF WE DO, FIFTY YEARS FROM NOW THE UNITED STATES OF AMERICA WILL BECOME AN IDENTICAL MICROCOSM OF THE ENTIRE WORLD. A HUNDRED COUNTRIES WILL EXIST WITHIN ONE. ALL OF THE PROBLEMS PEOPLE HAVE WITH EACH OTHER INTERNATIONALLY WILL THRIVE WITH FAR MORE EXTREME CONSEQUENCES; ALL IN THE SAME COUNTRY THAT THREE HUNDRED YEARS EARLIER OFFERED EVERYTHING, AND IN SO DOING, ENDED UP WITH NOTHING.

I SAY IT'S BETTER TO BACK OFF THIS ILLUSION OF ACCEPTANCE, AND CLEAN UP OUR DOMESTIC MESS. WE NEED TO DEVELOP AND INSTITUTE PROGRAMS THAT WILL, AT LEAST STRUCTURALLY, REBUILD IN A VERY SHORT PERIOD OF TIME THAT WHICH TOOK MUCH LONGER TO FALL APART. FOCUS HAS TO BE ON THE INNER CITIES. GENERAL SPECIFICS (OXYMORON) WILL BE MENTIONED IN SUBSEQUENT CHAPTERS.

ONCE WE HAVE OUR HOUSE IN ORDER, IT WOULD AGAIN BE POSSIBLE TO ASSIST OTHER PEOPLES WITHOUT INADVERTENTLY CONTRIBUTING TO A WORLD WITH NO HOPE; ONLY DARKNESS AND DESPAIR.

AMERICA SHOULD PLACE A TEN YEAR MORATORIUM ON IMMIGRATION. THE ONLY EXCEPTIONS WOULD BE THOSE INDIVIDUALS WHO, BY VIRTUE OF THEIR HUMAN OR LIVING RIGHTS INVOLVEMENT IN THEIR NATIVE COUNTRIES, ARE IN DANGER OF BEING KILLED.

CONCURRENT WITH THE NEW IMMIGRATION POLICY, THE NEW REQUIREMENTS FOR CONSIDERATION FOR IMMIGRATION NEEDS TO BE DISSEMINATED THROUGHOUT THE WORLD SO THAT THOSE WHO WISH TO BECOME AMERICAN CITIZENS WILL BE ABLE TO ACCOMMODATE THE NEW POLICY WITHIN THE TEN YEAR HIATUS.

PRINCIPAL AMONG THE REQUIREMENTS FOR IMMIGRATION IS THE ABILITY TO SPEAK ENGLISH WELL ENOUGH TO CONDUCT ALL MANNERS OF BUSINESS THAT NATURALLY OCCURS WHEN ONE MOVES TO A NEW COUNTRY. AN IMMIGRANT HAS GOT TO BE ABLE TO APPLY FOR WORK, GET A DRIVER'S LICENSE, A SOCIAL SECURITY

CARD, READ MAPS, SHOP, LOCATE SCHOOLS, HOSPITALS, AND UNDERSTAND THE LAW.

ONCE IMMIGRATION IS AGAIN ALLOWED, RESTRICTIONS WILL BE PLACED ON THE NUMBERS OF MEMBERS OF ONE FAMILY, A HEART BREAKING BUT NECESSARY PROVISION. IF A QUOTA DID NOT EXIST, ANY ELEMENT OF FAIRNESS OR ACCESS WOULD BE DENIED LARGE GROUPS OF PEOPLE, MOSTLY THE POOR OR DISENFRANCHISED. ONE OPTION COULD BECOME AN INTERNATIONAL LOTTERY; CAREFULLY SCRUTINIZED TO AVOID CHICANERY WITH DRAWINGS OCCURRING QUARTERLY.

WEALTHY, POLITICALLY CONNECTED FAMILIES WOULD MOVE THEIR ENTIRE ENTOURAGE TO AMERICA, GREAT GRAND PARENTS, GRAND PARENTS, PARENTS, ALL CHILDREN, AUNTS, UNCLES, ET AL, WHILE THOSE WHO HAVE SUFFERED THE MISFORTUNE OF A CHALLENGING BIRTHRIGHT, AND WHO DESPERATELY DESERVE AND NEED ACCESS TO THE DREAM, WILL BE DENIED BECAUSE THERE WILL BE NO MORE ROOM. WE HAVE BEEN WITNESSING THE VERY SAME THING FOR YEARS.

WEALTHY MIDDLE EASTERNERS, CHINESE, AND JAPANESE HAVE HAD VIRTUAL CARTE BLANCHE IN TERMS OF ENTRY INTO THE UNITED STATES. THEY PURCHASE UPSCALE HOMES IN EXCLUSIVE NEIGHBORHOODS, DRIVE LUXURY CARS, AND FRATERNIZE WITH THE VACUOUS TRENDIES, THUS CREATING A FALSE CLIMATE OF ACCEPTANCE. WHERE IS THEIR SENSE OF LOYALTY OR ATTACHMENT TO THEIR FELLOW COUNTRYMEN? HOW DID THEY ACQUIRE THEIR MONEY? IF THEY MADE IT BY EXPLOITING THEIR OWN PEOPLE, IF THEY ARE HEIRS TO THE FORTUNES OF SOMEONE WHO HAS, OR IF THEY RECEIVED THE MONEY AS A RESULT OF THE SALE OF THEIR BUSINESS, THEREBY DISPOSSESSING AND ABANDONING THEIR WORKERS, THEY ARE NO LONGER WELCOME TO MOVE TO AMERICA.

A MOTHER, FATHER, AND TWO CHILDREN CAN IMMIGRATE TO THE U.S. AS A FAMILY UNIT. ON ENTRY THEY MUST AGREE TO HAVE NO MORE CHILDREN, CONSISTENT WITH NEW POPULATION POLICY. NO EXCEPTIONS WILL BE MADE REGARDING EITHER NUMBERS OF FAMILY MEMBERS OR NUMBER OF CHILDREN.

All potential immigrants must pass a thorough physical examination to be conducted by U.S. Physicians, and all must provide an accurate family medical history.

No person with a criminal record will be allowed to immigrate. The only exceptions would be those who legitimately qualify as political prisoners.

All immigrants will be required to have enough money to support themselves and/or their family for one year based on a national average.

They all must prove that they have never been affiliated with a hate or repressive organization such as the Nazi's or were participants in policies such as apartheid.

Prospects must prove that they possess at least one marketable skill.

The head of the household, if the immigrants are a family unit, must be willing to move to a location in America where a demand exists for their skill.

Any person or company that exploits immigrants will be deported, among other sanctions.

All of the above requirements are necessary to insure and maintain a quality of life, one that can be shared by all. There is absolute strength in diversity. America in the ideal should appear to be a living collage of all the cultures on the Planet. People in concert should share their strengths and overcome their weaknesses. No one should be denied the right to perpetuate their cultures in art, education, custom, or ritual with the caveat that it is not done to the detriment of others.

There should be no more Diplomatic immunity allowed in the United States and our Diplomats should expect none elsewhere.

79

David Hayden

[No child whether legal or otherwise should be denied health care, food, housing, education, or clothing. Citizenship issues can be addressed during any evaluation procedure.]

The Political Process and Lobbying

"These less than complete people, public parasites all, saw only an opportunity to satisfy their egos and greed under the chameleonic costume of one who "aspires to public office"

Our founding Fathers and constitutional framers drafted a brilliant blueprint for democracy. Unfortunately, it was fatally flawed.

The constitutional authors had no idea that within 150 years, the Executive Branch of government, in concert with Congress, would serve exclusively the needs of the corporate community, or that by the mid 1900's; both would be owned by big business.

A century and one half ago the fantasies of fairness, equity, and parity only existed conceptually, and the proposition that all men are created equal and as such deserve equal treatment from birth (housing, education, health care, proper nutrition, etc.) was in fact a polemic placebo that could be righteously regurgitated at will by those seeking to placate the oppressed.

In fact, the only agenda those "good old boys" had was self serving and immediate, and had very little to do with the populace at large.

Ethnic people (American Indians, Afro-Americans, Chinese, Hispanic, et al) were not allowed to vote.

People who did not own property were not allowed to vote.

Women were not allowed to vote.

As a final safeguard against participation by the poor, poll taxes were introduced effectively making people pay

81

FOR WHAT WAS CLEARLY STATED IN "THE" DOCUMENT TO BE A GOD GIVEN RIGHT.

HELL, THE ONLY PEOPLE ALLOWED TO VOTE IN 1776 WERE CRONIES AND MEMBERS OF THE PREVAILING BODY POLITIC, OR WHITE MALES WITH BUCKS. VERY LITTLE OF WHAT WAS ORIGINALLY WRITTEN REGARDING THE POLITICAL BLUEPRINT FOR EQUAL RIGHTS AND REPRESENTATION HAD ANYTHING TO DO WITH EITHER NOBLE NOTION DURING THAT PERIOD IN OUR HISTORY.

THANKS TO THE STRUGGLES AND SUCCESSES OF BOTH THE CIVIL RIGHTS AND GENDER RIGHTS MOVEMENTS, MOST PEOPLE IN AMERICA NOW HAVE A VOTE. THE IRONY BEING THAT ALTHOUGH MOST ARE ABLE TO VOTE, THEY STILL HAVE VERY LITTLE CHOICE OR SAY CONCERNING THE COURSE OF THEIR COUNTRY.

TERM LIMITS:

REGARDING ASPIRANTS FOR OFFICE, THE WHOLE DEAL WAS SUPPOSED TO BE THAT AN INDIVIDUAL WOULD RUN FOR AN ELECTED OFFICE BECAUSE THAT PERSON WANTED TO PARTICIPATE IN A LARGER EFFORT TO IMPROVE THE QUALITY OF LIFE FOR HUMANS (AS OPPOSED TO ALL LIVING THINGS). THE IDEAL WAS WONDERFUL, THE NOTION GRAND THAT THESE PATRIOTS OOZING ALTRUISM AND WISDOM WOULD WEAVE INTO THE FABRIC OF OUR SOCIETY PROTECTION AND FAIRNESS, HOPE, ACCESS, AND OPPORTUNITY; THAT THESE WOULD BE LEADERS HEARD THE CALL, AND RESPONDED, FORSAKING FOR THAT MOMENT IN TIME, THEIR OWN SELF INTEREST.

WHAT A CROCK!

THESE LESS THAN COMPLETE PEOPLE, THESE PUBLIC PARASITES, SAW ONLY AN OPPORTUNITY TO SATISFY THEIR EGOS AND GREED UNDER THE CHAMELEONIC COSTUME OF ONE WHO "ASPIRES TO POLITICAL OFFICE".

TERM LIMITS NEED TO FEDERALLY MANDATED THAT APPLY NOT ONLY TO FEDERAL GOVERNMENT, BUT TO THE INDIVIDUAL STATES AS WELL.

THE PRESIDENT AND VICE-PRESIDENT CAN SERVE ONE SIX YEAR TERM.

THE VICE-PRESIDENT CAN RUN FOR ONE TERM AS PRESIDENT ONLY DURING THE ELECTION FOLLOWING HIS TENURE AS THE ASSISTANT EXECUTIVE.

SENATORS CAN SERVE ONE SIX YEAR TERM. THEY CAN RUN FOR PRESIDENT ONLY ONCE FOLLOWING THEIR TIME IN THE SENATE AND WOULD BE PROHIBITED FROM ACCEPTING ANY VICE-PRESIDENTIAL POSITION.

HOUSE MEMBERS COULD SERVE TWO FOUR YEAR TERMS AFTER WHICH THEY COULD MAKE A ONE TIME RUN FOR THE PRESIDENCY, BUT WOULD BE PROHIBITED FROM SEEKING OFFICE EITHER AS A SENATOR OR VICE-PRESIDENT.

NONE OF THE MEMBERS OF THE EXECUTIVE BRANCH OR CONGRESS CAN PARTICIPATE ONCE HIS/HER FINAL TERM EXPIRES.

CABINET APPOINTMENTS SHOULD REMAIN OUTSIDE THE TERM LIMIT RESTRICTIONS BUT SHOULD NOT EXCEED TWELVE YEARS.

PENSIONS RECEIVED AFTER SERVICE WOULD BE ADJUSTED TO REFLECT THOSE RECEIVED IN A COMPARABLE JOB IN THE PRIVATE SECTOR AND ONLY PAID AFTER AGE SIXTY-FIVE. POLITICIANS NEED TO BE REMINDED THAT THEY ARE IN FACT MEMBERS OF SOCIETY AND SHOULD BE ENCOURAGED TO REACQUAINT THEMSELVES WITH REAL AND REGULAR WORK.

NO MORE EXOTIC JUNKETS TO FOREIGN COUNTRIES WILL BE PAID FOR BY THE PUBLIC.

CHARACTER ISSUES: WE'VE GOT A WW11 VETERAN WHOSE PRIMARY POLITICAL PROP IS HIS INJURED ARM (WHEN THOUSANDS OF VETERAN PARAPLEGICS AND QUADRIPLEGICS NEVER COMPLAIN) RECEIVING A CITATION FROM A PRESIDENT WHOSE IDEA OF A THRILL IS TO PULL HIS PANTS DOWN AND ASK A STRANGER TO KISS HIS PEE PEE.

Campaign Finance and Reform:

Constitutional Authors had no way of knowing that the Industrial Revolution would produce corporate giants with resources of such size, that any distinction between corporate and national interest would disappear causing politicians to become the pawns of business and no longer representatives of the people.

In any large city in America, the cost of running for office prohibits anything more than token participation by most citizens residing in that community. As an example, the cost of waging a campaign for City Council in any metropolitan area with a population of 750,000 or more is a million bucks.

Candidates are seen only at well orchestrated rallies and functions, on television, or at fund raisers that require a financial contribution ($1,000 a plate dinners) far exceeding what any average American could afford.

Two things then happen. Politicians become the property of the affluent who seek to promote their own agenda(s), and the newly elected official quickly foregoes the notion of specific terms of office in lieu of the eminently more attractive "lifetime of service".

The benefits to these bureaucratic bimbos are obvious. Hobnob with the "rich and famous", receive outstanding salaries, the best health care, allowances for virtually everything, pensions for only serving a single term, and best of all, being constantly approached and pampered by lobbyists that promise and provide a lifestyle for the legislators family beyond any imaginable on purely the public dole.

There are a host of doable remedies available that would in effect return the country to it's citizenry in less than a generation. If only four were instituted now, they alone should provide enough momentum to carry the cause.

First, absolutely no campaign contributions are to be accepted from anyone or country outside the United States. Following that thought, no contributions will be accepted from anyone in the United States who is not a citizen. Anyone who attempts to circumvent the rule will be charged with a felony and all of his/her personal property will be seized. If the candidate is clearly involved, that person will be removed from the race. The proof will not have to be "beyond a reasonable doubt", the standard will be closer to that used in Civil Court i.e., if someone is dressed in the clothes of impropriety it's reasonable to conclude that they dance with rascals.

Secondly, all the major television networks will be required to provide equal FREE time to all qualified candidates; by qualified I mean those who have satisfied the petition requirements. After all, the networks think nothing about devoting hours to Simpson's slow speed chase; why not afford the same free air time to the rest of the aspiring crooks. Additionally the fee charged by municipalities to enter the race will be reduced so that it is affordable to everyone.

Thirdly, soft donations (no, I'm not talking about candidates or incumbents sexual congress), given directly to candidates cannot exceed $100.00 from any source. It will be a felony to circumvent the rule by forming political action committees (PACS) or other similar organizations. Every donation to a candidate must be in the form of a personal check made out to the candidate of a person's choice and cannot exceed one hundred dollars. Failure to abide by the rules could result in the forced withdrawal of the candidate from the election.

Hard money given to either the local or national arms of the respective parties, cannot exceed $50,000 with the codicil that all the dollars directed toward a specific candidate be matched with the others in the party. If candidate A receives $20,000, then candidates B, C, etc. should receive the same amount. We need to encourage

A RETREAT FROM THE ALLURE OF LARGE AND EASY MONEY AND A RETURN TO GRASSROOTS POLITICS. GO TO MEETINGS, KNOCK ON DOORS, PUT SIGNS ON CORNERS AND IN PICK-UPS, HAVE A PLANE TRAIL A BANNER, DO MORE RADIO, RIDE A HORSE, TEAM UP WITH OTHER CANDIDATES TO PROMOTE THE COMMON AGENDA, GET BACK TO THE UNIFYING CONCEPT OF "WE ARE ONE", AND/OR JUST GET BACK TO RELIANCE ON CREATIVITY AND IMAGINATION RATHER THAN PRESENTING DECEPTIVE AND PHONY IMAGES ON TV.

AND FOURTH, ANY AND ALL CAMPAIGN SPENDING WILL BE LIMITED TO THAT OF THE OPPOSING CANDIDATE WITH THE LEAST MONEY. IN CALIFORNIA FOR INSTANCE, IF PAUL THE PLUMBER FROM VISALIA IS RUNNING AGAINST HEMORRHOID HUFFINGTON, THE ROID WILL BE ALLOWED TO SPEND ONLY AS MUCH MONEY AS PAUL . IF THE ROID WANTED TO DONATE SOME OF HIS INHERITED MONEY TO PAUL SO THAT HE COULD SPEND MORE HIMSELF, THAT'S COOL, BUT ABSENT THAT, NO CANDIDATE IN ANY ELECTION WILL BE ALLOWED TO SPEND MORE THAN THEIR POOREST OPPONENT.

THE PENALTY FOR VIOLATING ANY OF THESE RULES WOULD BE REMOVAL FROM THE RACE WITH THE ADDITIONAL REQUIREMENT THAT THE OFFENDING CANDIDATE REPAY ANY AND ALL MONEY HE'D RECEIVED FROM OUTSIDE SOURCES.

LOBBYING:

THERE ARE CLOSE TO ONE HUNDRED LOBBYISTS FOR EVERY FEDERAL LEGISLATOR IN AMERICA TODAY BY THE GOVERNMENTS OWN RECKONING. THEY ARE THE BACILLUS OF BIG BUSINESS.

PREYING ON THE WORST IN HUMAN NATURE, THESE CORPORATE EVANGELISTS PREACH THE GOSPEL OF THEIR OWNERS, THE CONSCIOUS LESS CEO'S AND BOARDS OF DIRECTORS RESPONSIBLE FOR PROFITS ABOVE EVERYTHING ELSE. THEY INFLUENCE THE LEGISLATORS WITH EVERY CONCEIVABLE KIND OF GIFT OR GRATUITY, MOST OFTEN IN WAYS NOT EASILY TRACED I.E.: A CHILD'S COLLEGE TUITION, PRE-PAID VACATIONS, USE OF CORPORATE JETS AND LUXURY AUTOMOBILES, CASH, ETC. MANY CONGRESSIONAL VETERANS BEGIN TO RELY ON A CERTAIN STANDARD OF LIVING THAT THE FRIENDLY AND MULTI-FACETED ASSISTANCE PROVIDES.

REMOVE THE LOBBYISTS AND YOU REMOVE ONE OF THE MAJOR INCENTIVES TO REMAIN IN OFFICE.

LOBBYING SHOULD BE A FELONY.

IF AN INDIVIDUAL IS CAUGHT INFLUENCE PEDDLING HE/SHE WOULD HAVE THE MAJORITY OF THEIR ASSETS SEIZED AND BE INCARCERATED IN A MINIMUM SECURITY FACILITY FROM WHERE THEY WOULD BE REQUIRED TO ENTER THE COMMUNITY DAILY AND LABOR AT PUBLIC WORKS PROJECTS REBUILDING THE INFRASTRUCTURE.

THE CORPORATIONS THAT HIRED THE CREEPS WOULD BE FINED THE ENTIRE EQUIVALENT OF THEIR BEST'S YEAR'S PROFITS. THE CEO'S AND BOARDS OF DIRECTORS WOULD BE FINED THE EQUIVALENT OF THEIR MOST RECENT YEARS SALARY AND BE REQUIRED FORFEIT 75% OF THEIR PERSONAL ASSETS.

ONCE AGAIN, ANY POLICING OR INVESTIGATION OF LOBBYING ACTIVITY WOULD BE PAID FOR WITH THE FINES AND ASSETS SEIZED.

MILITARY SERVICE

"FAR TOO MANY INDIVIDUALS CAMPAIGNING FOR OR ELECTED TO PUBLIC OFFICE HAVE NEVER SERVED IN THE ARMED FORCES OF THE UNITED STATES OF AMERICA. PROOF OF TIME SERVED SHOULD BE A REQUIREMENT OF ALL CANDIDATES ASPIRING TO BE AMERICA'S PRESIDENT"

MANDATORY SERVICE:

ALL PHYSICALLY ABLE MEN AND WOMEN SHOULD BE REQUIRED TO SPEND TWO YEARS IN THE SERVICE OF THEIR COUNTRY.

GIVEN THE EXTRAORDINARILY LARGE NUMBER OF CHALLENGES FACING TODAY'S YOUTH, MILITARY SERVICE WOULD PROVIDE A FOUNDATION FOR THEIR FUTURE AS ADULTS. EVEN AS LATE AS THE TURN OF THE CENTURY, FAMILY UNITS SUPPLIED MUCH OF THE COHESIVENESS AND DISCIPLINE NECESSARY TO TAKE THE STEP FROM CHILD TO ADULT. OVER FIFTY PER CENT OF ALL FAMILIES LACK A RESIDENT FATHER. MORE ALARMING STILL IS THE FACT THAT OVER FIFTY PER CENT OF GRANDPARENTS ARE RAISING THEIR CHILDREN'S CHILDREN AT LEAST PART TIME. MTV AND VH-1, XBOX, SEGA, AND FANTASY PIXELS RAISE OUR CHILDREN ON "MAKE BELIEVE".

MILITARY SERVICE WOULD BE THAT THIRD GREEN WIRE PROVIDING THE GROUND FOR OUR TATTOOED, PIERCED, POST PUBESCENT CITIZENS.

CONSCRIPTION WILL TRAIN OUR YOUTH USING THE TOOLS AND TECHNIQUES NECESSARY TO DEFEND OUR COUNTRY AGAINST AN INCREASINGLY LARGE NUMBER OF DIFFERENT ENEMIES, BOTH FOREIGN AND DOMESTIC.

THE MONEY CURRENTLY USED FOR RECRUITING CAN BE PUT TO BETTER USE.

WE REMAIN A PRIMITIVE SPECIES. WE NEED TO KNOW HOW TO DEFEND OURSELVES IN EVERYDAY LIFE, AND OUR COUNTRY SHOULD IT BECOME NECESSARY.

CONSCIENTIOUS OBJECTORS CAN BE ASSIGNED PEACEFUL DUTY IN ADMINISTRATION, MEDICAL, OR SUPPLY DESIGNATIONS WITHOUT COMPROMISING THEIR BELIEF. IF THAT IS UNACCEPTABLE TO THEM, THEY CAN EXPATRIATE TO ANOTHER COUNTRY.

WAR IS A REALITY AND IT WILL BECOME MORE SO. NO ONE SAVE A DEMENTED SOUL ENJOYS OR ENCOURAGES CONFLICT. NO ONE HAS THE RIGHT TO EXPECT OR DEMAND THAT ANOTHER PERSON RISK LIFE AND LIMB SO THAT THEY CAN REAP THE REWARD. MAKE NO MISTAKE ABOUT IT; THE REWARD IS FREEDOM. WE CAN SAY ANYTHING, DO MOST ANYTHING, AND RELOCATE ANYWHERE AND AS OFTEN AS WE WISH. OUR RIGHT TO WORSHIP IS PROTECTED AS IS OUR RIGHT NOT TO WORSHIP.

ALL OF THOSE LIBERTIES AND MORE HAVE TO BE PROTECTED. IT IS PATENTLY UNFAIR FOR ANY AMERICAN CITIZEN TO PLACE THAT BURDEN ON ANOTHER.

MAKE THE SACRIFICE AND THEN COMPLAIN TO YOUR HEART'S CONTENT; YOUR RIGHT TO DO THAT IS GUARANTEED BY OUR CONSTITUTION.

National Defense and the CIA

"Area 51-The area should be declassified for another reason which is more than simply shared information or knowledge; concentrated power as it exists in that desert is extremely dangerous to a Democracy"

National Defense:

Make no mistake about it; the United States of America must remain globally militarily dominant. Despite the end of the "Cold War" and the accompanying dissolution of the Soviet Union, the emerging and growing nuclear capabilities of Asian and Middle Eastern countries requires us to maintain our position at the forefront of the fray in terms of both weapons technology and delivery systems.

Threats to international peace and freedom will not only continue, but increase from volatile and unstable sources around the world. Two very probable scenarios spring to mind.

The economies of countries run by corrupt and incompetent men will eventually completely collapse. Any military capability that did exist will be appropriated by the despots and used indiscriminately in the pursuit of their personal agendas. America should be especially interested in the possibility of an overt action emerging from the chaos and anarchy which could directly cause harm to the United States or its citizens.

Another consideration might be that military intervention may be necessary should the general failure of a countries social and economic system threaten the stability of the free world.

The time has long past when we can afford to coddle and cajole Dictators and their cronies.

ALL OF THEM, THE MOMMAR KHADAFY'S, THE HAFEZ ASSAD'S, THE AYATOLLAH'S, THE IDI AMIN'S, THE SADAM HUSSEIN'S, ALONG WITH THE REMAINDER OF THE EVIL RULERS, SHOULD HAVE BEEN EXCISED FROM EARTH LONG AGO AS WOULD BE ANY INFECTED BOIL FROM AN OTHERWISE HEALTHY BODY.

IF AT ALL POSSIBLE, RELIANCE ON AIR SUPERIORITY AND STRATEGY SHOULD BE FIRST PRIORITY IN ANY ARMED ENGAGEMENT. WE WANT TO USE OUR BRAINS AND OUR BOMBS NOT OUR BOYS AND THEIR BRAWN. UNFORTUNATELY, GROUND TROOPS WILL STILL BE NECESSARY IN TWO SITUATIONS, ONE FOREIGN AND THE OTHER DOMESTIC.

FOLLOWING ANY COMPREHENSIVE AIR STRIKE MARINE AND/OR ARMY PERSONNEL WILL HAVE TO MOP UP AND ESTABLISH CONTROL OF THE TARGET AREA. TANKS ALONG WITH OTHER ARMORED PERSONNEL CARRIERS SHOULD BE USED TO PROTECT THE TROOPS WHENEVER POSSIBLE. THE TERM "LIMITED ENGAGEMENT " SHOULD BE EXPANDED TO MEAN THAT ALL FORCE NECESSARY TO ACHIEVE A CERTAIN OBJECTIVE WILL BE USED REGARDLESS OF CASUALTIES IN AN EFFORT TO SPARE U. S. FORCE'S LIVES. FOR EXAMPLE, IF INTELLIGENCE HAS INDISPUTABLE EVIDENCE THAT SADAM HUSSEIN IS HIDING IN A SPECIFIC LOCATION BUT THE TARGET IS SURROUNDED BY CIVILIANS (AS IS HIS MO), THAN THE GREATER GOOD MUST PREVAIL. AS I AM CONVINCED THAT TRUMAN MADE THE CORRECT, ALBEIT TRAGIC, DECISION TO DROP ATOMIC BOMBS RATHER THAN RISK TENS OF THOUSANDS MORE AMERICAN AND JAPANESE LIVES WITH AN INVASION, I AM SURE THAT THE ELIMINATION OF THE BAD APPLE HUSSEIN WOULD JUSTIFY LOSING THE TREE IN LIEU OF THE WHOLE ORCHARD.

SPEAKING OF CROPS, AIR POWER SHOULD BE AGGRESSIVELY USED TO ERADICATE DRUG PRODUCTION IN FOREIGN COUNTRIES. AS INDICATED IN THE DRUG CHAPTER, USE OF CHOPPERS, FIGHTERS, AND MISSILES IS APPROPRIATE GIVEN THE CORRUPT AND FAILED EFFORTS OF THOSE RUNNING THEIR RESPECTIVE COUNTRIES. FUNNELING BILLIONS OF DOLLARS INTO THE POCKETS OF THOSE IMPOSTORS DOES NOTHING TO ELIMINATE THE PROBLEM.

ONCE AGAIN, ALL THIS WOULD NOT BE NECESSARY IF WE DIDN'T BEHAVE LIKE PRIMITIVE AND PREDATORY ANIMALS USING LESS THAN THREE PERCENT OF OUR BRAINS.

NO MATTER WHAT MILITARY ACTIVITY THE UNITED STATES MIGHT BE INVOLVED IN, WE WILL LEAVE NO TROOPS EITHER ON THE BATTLEFIELD OR AS HOSTAGES IN SOME OTHER LOCATION. WE NEED TO BE PREPARED TO EXTRACT OUR MEN IMMEDIATELY WITH NO QUARTER GIVEN.

THE UNITED STATES SHOULD NOT BE INVOLVED IN ANY WAY WITH CHEMICAL WEAPONS DEVELOPMENT. IF A MILITARY MISSION IS INEVITABLE, TROOPS SHOULD NOT BE SENT INTO COMBAT SITUATIONS WHERE A CHEMICAL THREAT EXISTS. IN THAT INSTANCE, NOTICE SHOULD BE GIVEN OUR ADVERSARY THAT UNLESS THAT COUNTRY'S CHEMICAL WEAPONS ARE DESTROYED WITHIN A RAPID TIME FRAME; THEY WILL BE ANNIHILATED WITH AIR POWER.

THE OTHER SITUATION WHERE GROUND TROOPS WILL BE INCREASINGLY RELIED ON TO RESTORE AND MAINTAIN ORDER WILL BE DURING DOMESTIC RIOTS AND CIVIL WAR. UNLESS RADICAL AND RAPIDLY EMPLOYED SOCIAL CHANGE OCCURS WITHIN THE NEXT GENERATION, THE UNITED STATES WILL BEGIN TO EXPERIENCE CIVIL UNREST UNPARALLELED SINCE THE CIVIL WAR. THE ANARCHY WILL ASSUME THE SHAPE OF THE MULTI-HEADED MEDUSA. ACTS OF TERRORISM WILL NO LONGER BE RESTRICTED TO "FANATICAL" ELEMENTS FROM THE MIDDLE EAST OR ELSEWHERE. INNER CITY ETHNIC UPHEAVAL, THE RUPTURE OF THE GROSSLY INEQUITABLE CLASS SYSTEM (RICH VS. POOR, HAVES VS. HAVE NOT'S), THE OVERT ACTS OF TERROR BY THE NEW MILITIAS (OKLAHOMA BOMBING), ALONG WITH THAT INDIVIDUAL IN SOCIETY WHO IS POTENTIALLY MORE DESTRUCTIVE THAN ALL THE OTHERS, THE LONE WOLF OR LOOSE CANNON, WILL ACT INDEPENDENTLY OF EACH OTHER TO CREATE CHAOS ON A GRAND SCALE.

ALL ARMED FORCES GROUND TROOPS NEED TO BE TRAINED AND EQUIPPED TO DEAL WITH CIVIL WAR. STRATEGIES NEED TO BE DEVELOPED, NEW KINDS OF NON LETHAL WEAPONS NEED TO BE DESIGNED, AND ALL CITIZENS OF AMERICA NEED TO BE INFORMED OF THE PROBABILITY AND DANGER SO THAT FAMILIES

CAN FORMULATE SOME KIND OF PERSONAL SAFETY PLAN SHOULD THEY BE CAUGHT IN A THREATENING SITUATION.

WOMEN SHOULD NOT BE ALLOWED TO FUNCTION AS FOOT SOLDIERS OR MAN THE FRONT LINES IN ANY COMBAT ENVIRONMENT. WOMEN CAN FLY PLANES, COMMAND SHIPS, AND PERFORM ANY OF THE MULTITUDES OF OTHER ADMINISTRATIVE AND/OR MANAGERIAL TASKS INVOLVED IN MILITARY OPERATIONS. ACCORDINGLY, THE PHYSICAL FITNESS STANDARDS FOR ALL RECRUITS AND REGULAR DUTY PERSONNEL SHOULD BE RAISED BACK TO PREVIOUS LEVELS.

TWO THINGS REGARDING COST RELATED TO ALL ITEMS MILITARY.

THE ACQUISITION OF NEW "BIG TICKET" WEAPONS NEEDS TO MORE ACCURATELY RELATE TO ANY REAL THREAT, ALWAYS WITH AN EYE TO THE FUTURE. WE ALREADY POSSESS ENOUGH ROCKET DRIVEN FIREPOWER TO DESTROY THE WORLD MANY TIMES OVER. SHIT, AFTER THE FIRST OR SECOND STRIKE THE REST BECOMES IRRELEVANT. OUR NATIONAL FOCUS SHOULD NOW SHIFT TO DEVELOPING WEAPONS AND DELIVERY SYSTEMS THAT COULD COMFORTABLY BE CONSIDERED ADEQUATE FOR THE ENTIRE TWENTY FIRST CENTURY, WHILE INCORPORATING EXISTING ARSENALS INTO THE EQUATION. GIVEN THE EXTENT OF GLOBAL SOCIAL UNREST, ONE MIGHT REASONABLY DEDUCE THAT MOST COUNTRIES ARE BECOMING TOO PREOCCUPIED WITH THE AFFAIRS OF THEIR OWN HOUSE, WITHOUT TAKING ON THE NEIGHBORS.

A SECOND AND VERY USEFUL FUNCTION OF THE "NEW" WEAPONS SHOULD BE DIRECTED TOWARD USE AS AN ANTI METEOR OR ASTEROID DEVICE. SINCE THE FOCUS OF MUCH OF OUR SCIENTIFIC ENERGY IS GOING TO BE DIRECTED TOWARD SPACE, COMMON SENSE WOULD INDICATE THAT WHEREVER POSSIBLE WE SHOULD DEVELOP SOME REACTIONARY DEFENSE TO ROGUE GALACTIC THREATS.

NONE OF THE GOODS PURCHASED FOR USE IN THE MILITARY SHOULD COST MORE THAN CIVILIANS PAY AT A RETAIL OUTLET. THE WASTE INHERENT IN THE PURCHASING ARM OF THE PENTAGON IS LEGENDARY. A SEPARATE AND INDEPENDENT CIVILIAN ACCOUNTING FIRM SHOULD PERFORM A COMPLETE AND COMPREHENSIVE AUDIT OF THE SUPPLY/PURCHASING DEPARTMENT OF THE ARMED

FORCES. ONCE THE EXTENT OF THE MALFEASANCE IS EVIDENT, THOSE RESPONSIBLE SHOULD BE DEALT WITH QUICKLY AND WITH NO MERCY. NEXT, A COMPANY FROM THE PRIVATE SECTOR THAT IS LARGE ENOUGH TO HANDLE THE TASK SHOULD BE AWARDED THE CONTRACT FOR BUYING, STORING, AND SHIPPING OF ALL MILITARY NON WEAPONS RELATED GOODS.

TANTAMOUNT TO THE SUCCESS OF THE EFFORT IS THE NEED TO EXAMINE ALL THE INVENTORIES OF EXISTING SUPPLIES (SOME GOING BACK TO WWII), SHITCAN WHAT IS NO LONGER SAFE, TRANSPORT ALL OTHER FOOD, BEDDING, CLOTHING, ETC. THAT IS SALVAGEABLE (BUT NO LONGER USEFUL TO THE MILITARY) TO PEOPLE IN AMERICA THAT NEED IT, AND USE THE EXCESS OF "HARD" ITEMS (TOILETS, SINKS, LIGHT OR PLUMBING FIXTURES, DOORS, HARDWARE, CABINETS, ETC.) TO ASSIST PEOPLE INVOLVED IN REBUILDING THE INNER CITIES.

NOT A SINGLE NEW ITEM PURCHASED FOR MILITARY OR GOVERNMENT USE SHALL EXCEED NORMAL CIVILIAN COST.

ALL CONTRACTS FOR 'BIG TICKET" ITEMS SUCH AS PLANES, CHOPPERS, OR SHIPS, WILL BE FLEXIBLE IN TERMS OF QUANTITY. THE CONGRESSIONAL APPROPRIATION SHOULD REFLECT THE "AS MANY AS" PART OF THE CONTRACT WITH THE UNDERSTANDING THAT ONLY THE "NO FEWER THAN" WILL BE WRITTEN IN STONE. THIS SHOULD BE DONE SO THAT MONEY WILL BE AVAILABLE TO ASSIST U. S. CITIZENS IN TIMES OF NATURAL DISASTER OR CIVIL UNREST. FOR INSTANCE, IF THE 1996 FLOODS IN THE MIDWEST RESULTED IN TWO BILLION DOLLARS IN UNANTICIPATED DAMAGE (NOTHING IN THE ANNUAL BUDGET OR FEDERAL RESERVES TO COVER), THE CANCELLATION OF ONE BOMBER ALONG WITH A COUPLE OF CHOPPERS WOULD ALLOW QUICK FINANCIAL ASSISTANCE TO THOSE WHO DESPERATELY NEED IT. IT'S SIMPLE AND IT MAKES SENSE.

THERE WILL NO SALES OF MAJOR WEAPONS TO NON ALLIED COUNTRIES.

AREA 51 SHOULD BECOME PUBLIC IMMEDIATELY. THE ANTIQUATED ARGUMENT THAT COMMUNIST REGIMES SO OFTEN USED "THE PUBLIC CAN'T HANDLE THE TRUTH" CAN NO LONGER BE USED, AT LEAST IN THIS REGARD. THE AREA SHOULD BE DECLASSIFIED

FOR ANOTHER REASON WHICH IS MORE IMPORTANT THAN SIMPLY SHARED INFORMATION OR KNOWLEDGE, CONCENTRATED POWER AS IT EXISTS IN THAT DESERT IS EXTREMELY DANGEROUS TO A DEMOCRACY.

CIA:

SNOOPING IS UNFORTUNATELY A BY PRODUCT OF THE PARANOIA AND LUNACY THAT PERMEATES OUR SOCIETY. VERY FEW PEOPLE KNOW MUCH ABOUT THE ORGANIZATION. TWO IMMEDIATE ACTIONS ARE NECESSARY TO DEFINE AND CONTAIN THE CLANDESTINE STRUCTURE.

WE NEED TO RE-EVALUATE THE NEED FOR LARGE NUMBERS OF FIELD AGENTS IN THE TWENTY FIRST CENTURY IN LIGHT OF THE NEW AND EXTREMELY SENSITIVE SURVEILLANCE TECHNOLOGY. A LOT OF THE SPYING THAT COULD ONLY BE DONE BY A PERSON CAN NOW BE DONE BY A DEVICE. HALF THE NUMBER OF FIELD AGENTS IN THE CIA SHOULD BE TRANSFERRED TO THE FBI WHERE THEIR SERVICES AND EXPERIENCE CAN BE PUT TO GOOD USE DEALING WITH INEVITABLE CIVIL UNREST. I FEEL FAIRLY COMFORTABLE WITH THE NOTION THAT THE CIA WOULD RATHER AVOID SCRUTINY BY ITS BOSSES (CITIZENS OF THE U.S.) AT ALL COSTS. REMOVING THEIR VEIL OF SECRECY IS SYNONYMOUS WITH RELINQUISHING POWER, TWO CONCEPTS WHICH OFTEN GRACE THE SAME STAGE.

SINCE WE NO LONGER PERCEIVE A THREAT FROM ABROAD, THERE IS DEFINITELY NO NEED FOR AN OPEN ENDED BUDGET. WITH SOME DEGREE OF SECURITY, THE AGENCY SHOULD HAVE TO JUSTIFY THEIR EXPENDITURES AT LEAST TO THE NATIONAL SECURITY COUNCIL.

THE CIA AS A SEPARATE ENTITY OR BRANCH OF GOVERNMENT SHOULD CEASE TO EXIST IN TEN YEARS. IT IS TIME TO QUIT PLAYING COWBOY WITH SPECIAL OPERATIONS AND CERTAINLY TIME TO INSURE THAT INCIDENTS SUCH AS IRAN/CONTRA ALONG WITH THE SELLING OF DRUGS TO AMERICANS IN ORDER TO FINANCE CLANDESTINE EFFORTS, CEASES. IT IS UNBELIEVABLE THAT A BRANCH OF GOVERNMENT ENTRUSTED WITH AMERICA'S SECURITY WOULD RESORT TO PUSHING CRACK AND COCAINE BECAUSE

THEY KNEW THAT CONGRESS WOULD NOT GO ALONG WITH THEIR PROGRAM, AND WOULD NEVER FUND SAME.

ATF AND DEA:

THERE IS NO EFFECTIVE DRUG ENFORCEMENT OCCURRING WITHIN THE INFLUENCE OF THE UNITED STATES GOVERNMENT, THERE IS A WHOLE LOT OF WASTED MONEY ON WHAT AMOUNTS TO INTERNATIONAL BRIBERY, BUDGETS, AND SALARIES OF PERSONNEL WITH NO PURPOSE.

AS STATED BEFORE, THE STATE DEPT. IN CONJUNCTION WITH THE MILITARY SHOULD HANDLE ALL DRUG RELATED CONSIDERATIONS BEYOND OUR BORDERS.

BOTH ALCOHOL AND TOBACCO ARE DRUGS. THE ATF SHOULD MERGE WITH THE DEA RESULTING IN OBVIOUS ADVANTAGES. THE NEW SINGLE AGENCY SHOULD CONCENTRATE THEIR EFFORTS ON DOMESTIC DRUG LAW ENFORCEMENT AND TERRORISM.

ALL SECURITY AND ENFORCEMENT AGENCIES SHOULD SHARE ONE, CENTRAL INFORMATION SOURCE WHICH IN TURN WOULD PROVIDE ALL LAW ENFORCEMENT AGENCIES IN AMERICA WITH DATA CONCERNING ALL ILLEGAL ACTIVITY IN THE COUNTRY. THIS WOULD BE PARTICULARLY USEFUL REGARDING MISSING CHILDREN, AND CHILD ABUSERS.

CONSOLIDATION, NOT SEPARATION SHOULD BECOME THE OPERATIVE BYWORD IN GOVERNMENT. TOO MANY DISCONNECTED BRANCHES WITH TOO MANY HIDDEN AGENDAS MAKE FOR A VERY WEIGHTY TREE.

RACE RELATIONS

"NOW THE ONLY REMINDER OF THE FREEDOM OF MOVEMENT THEY ONCE ENJOYED AS A BIRTHRIGHT CAN BE SEEN FROM A ROADSIDE STAND ON THE OUTSKIRTS OF THEIR RESERVATION AS A WINNEBAGO RV ROLLS BY"

RACISM IS ALIVE AND WELL IN AMERICA AND THE WORLD.

GIVEN THE PRIMITIVE NATURE OF THE HUMAN ANIMAL, IT PROBABLY ALWAYS WILL BE. SO THE QUESTION IS HOW TO DEAL WITH IT, SINCE IN THE NEAR FUTURE WE WON'T BE ABLE TO ELIMINATE THE DISEASE.

THE FIRST STRIKE AGAINST THIS CRUEL NONSENSE MUST BE MADE IN THE FORM OF A MASSIVE COMMITMENT OF MONEY TO THE INNER CITIES. CURRENT INNER CITIES ARE IN REALITY INNER SLUMS. DEPENDING ON WHICH CITY YOU TARGET, 25 TO 55% OF ALL INHABITANTS OF THE PROJECTS ARE ON SOME KIND OF PUBLIC ASSISTANCE WHETHER IT IS IN THE FORM OF WELFARE, HUD, SSI, OR ATD. OVER ONE MILLION YOUNG BLACK MEN ARE IN PRISONS AND THAT NUMBER IS RISING RAPIDLY. THE MAJORITY OF YOUNG PEOPLE DO NOT FINISH HIGH SCHOOL. THE INCIDENCE OF TEENAGE PREGNANCY IS EPIDEMIC. ETHNIC COLLEGE STUDENT'S ENROLMENTS ARE DROPPING PER CAPITA. THOSE MINORITIES WHO HAVE MANAGED TO MAKE IT INTO THE MAINSTREAM ARE HAMPERED IN THEIR UPWARD MOBILITY BY A VERY REAL AND NOT SO TRANSPARENT "GLASS CEILING". IT ISN'T ANY WAY TO LIVE FOR ANY HUMAN BEING.

SYSTEMATICALLY, THE BUILDINGS IN THE INNER SLUMS NEED TO BE RAZED AND REBUILT. NEW SCHOOLS STAFFED BY TRUE PROFESSIONALS NEED TO BE BUILT ON SITE. COMPREHENSIVE MEDICAL CENTERS SHOULD BE CONSTRUCTED IN THE IMMEDIATE NEIGHBORHOOD. THE HEALTH CARE FACILITIES SHOULD INCLUDE COMPLETE PRE NATAL CARE, DRUG AND REHAB DEPARTMENTS, A MENTAL HEALTH AND COUNSELING WING, AND A TRAUMA UNIT.

PART AND PARCEL OF EITHER THE COLLECTIVE COMMUNITY EFFORT OR AN INDIVIDUAL'S ATTEMPT TOWARD SELF IMPROVEMENT

IS THE RESURRECTION OF THE SURROUNDING ENVIRONMENT. A PERSON ALWAYS FEELS BETTER WHEN THEY ARE CLEANLY AND NEATLY CLOTHED AND/OR LIVE IN A SAFE AND SANITARY HOME. REPLACING SOME OF THE PHYSICAL DRESSING AROUND ONE'S LIFE WILL GO A LONG WAY TOWARD IMPROVING A PERSON'S SELF ESTEEM.

PART OF THE PROCESS WILL INVOLVE A KIND OF SOCIAL TRIAGE SIMILAR TO THAT EMPLOYED IN THE HOMELESSNESS CHAPTER. A TRAGIC BUT NECESSARY FACT IS THAT UNLESS THE CHAFF IS SEPARATED FROM THE WHEAT, THE EFFORT WILL NOT STAND A CHANCE. THOSE INDIVIDUALS THAT DO NOT WANT TO OR ARE UNPREPARED MENTALLY OR EMOTIONALLY TO ATTEMPT INDEPENDENT AND RESPONSIBLE LIVING WILL JOIN THOSE IN ONE OF THE THREE ESTABLISHED INSTITUTIONS PROVIDED FOR THE HOMELESS.

THE CRIMINAL POPULATION IN THE PROJECTS WILL BE DEALT WITH ACCORDING TO DICTUM IN CRIME AND PUNISHMENT.

THOSE REMAINING IN THE RENOVATED INNER CITIES WILL NOT HAVE TO WORRY ABOUT MONEY. THEY WILL HAVE TO GO TO SCHOOL AND PASS COURSES THAT HAVE THE SAME STANDARD AS THE REST OF THE ACADEMIC COMMUNITY. THEY WILL HAVE TO ACCEPT VOCATIONAL TRAINING ACCORDING TO A COMBINATION OF TESTING AND THEIR PERSONAL INTERESTS. ALL OF THE OTHER EXTERNAL SOCIAL SANCTIONS OR LAWS WILL APPLY EQUALLY IN THE NEW INNER CITIES.

THE GOAL OF THE WHOLE ENTERPRISE IS SELF SUFFICIENCY. TO ACCOMPLISH THAT, OTHER SOCIAL PROGRAMS MUST REMAIN IN PLACE.

AFFIRMATIVE ACTION:

IT IS IMPERATIVE THAT AFFIRMATIVE ACTION CONTINUE TO BE INCLUDED IN THE SCHOOLS AND WORKPLACES OF AMERICA. IT IS EQUALLY IMPORTANT THAT THE STANDARDS OF EXCELLENCE BE ELEVATED TO THEIR ORIGINAL LEVELS. NOTHING COULD BE MORE SELF DEFEATING THAN REQUIRING MINORITY HIRING OR ADMITTANCE BASED ON REDUCED QUALIFICATIONS. THE FOCUS ON

IMPROVED EDUCATIONAL TOOLS AND TEACHING WILL EVENTUALLY CHANGE THE PERCEIVED NEED FOR THAT.

AS PREVIOUSLY STATED, THE REAL WORK NEEDS TO BE DONE IN THE COMMUNITIES IN WHICH ETHNIC MINORITIES LIVE. ONLY BY PROVIDING PARALLEL LIVING CONDITIONS ALONG WITH EQUAL HEALTH CARE AND HOUSING WILL ANYONE HAVE AN OPPORTUNITY TO ACQUIRE THE SAME KNOWLEDGE AND SKILLS REQUIRED IN THE VOCATIONAL MARKETPLACE.

THE NEW EMPHASIS OR FOCUS OF AFFIRMATIVE ACTION SHOULD BE ON THE PHYSICAL REBUILDING AND RECLAMATION OF THE INNER CITIES IN COMBINATION WITH THE RESURRECTION OF THE INNER CITY'S SOULS.

THE WELL INTENTIONED ARCHITECTS OF AFFIRMATIVE ACTION MADE THE MISTAKE OF CHOOSING THE EASY AND AVAILABLE PATH OF STANDARDS REDUCTION WHILE IGNORING OUR CONTINUING METROPOLITAN DECAY. FIX THE FOUNDATION AND YOU RIGHT THE BUILDING.

A FORM OF WELFARE WILL PROBABLY HAVE TO REMAIN IN EFFECT FOR THE FORESEEABLE FUTURE, WHICH TRANSLATES INTO THE NEXT COUPLE OF CENTURIES. THERE WILL ALWAYS BE A NUMBER OF PEOPLE WHO FOR ANY NUMBER OF REASONS WILL NEVER FUNCTION IN SOCIETY. THE HUMANE AND PROPER THING TO DO IS CARE FOR THEM WITHOUT RESTRICTING THEIR ACCESS TO ANY OF THE RIGHTS OR PRIVILEGES THE REST OF SOCIETY ENJOYS.

THE WHOLE IDEA IS THAT ONCE A FORM OF PARITY IS ACHIEVED, THE SEPARATION BETWEEN THE INNER CITY AND THE REST OF THE COMMUNITY WILL CEASE TO EXIST THROUGH A FORM OF SOCIAL OSMOSIS AND ASSIMILATION.

THAT OF COURSE WILL NOT ELIMINATE RACISM BUT IT WILL AT LEAST MITIGATE THE IMPACT.

I WOULD LIKE TO SEE ALL OF THE RACES INTER MARRY. THE CHILDREN WOULD BE BEAUTIFUL AND BRIGHT, POSSESSING THE BEST OF BOTH GENES. THAT IN AND OF ITSELF WOULD NOT

UNFORTUNATELY PREVENT DISCRIMINATION, BUT IT WOULD GO A LONG WAY TOWARD CHANGING ITS COMPLEXION.

THERE SHOULD BE NO MORE PATIENCE ALLOWED THOSE ORGANIZATIONS WHO PRACTICE INTOLERANCE AND HATE. OUTFITS LIKE THE KKK AND WHITE ARYAN NATION (OR SIMILAR COUNTERPARTS), SHOULD NO LONGER BE ALLOWED TO HOLD PUBLIC RALLIES AND MARCHES. THEY WILL NO LONGER BE PERMITTED TO PASS OUT LITERATURE IN THE COMMUNITY. IF ANY MEMBER OF A HATE GROUP VIOLATES THE LAW, THEY WILL GO TO JAIL FOR A MINIMUM TEN YEARS FOR THE FIRST OFFENCE. PENALTIES FOR THE SECOND INFRACTION WILL INCLUDE LIFE WITH POSSIBILITY OF PAROLE AND SEIZURE OF ALL ASSETS. AFTER THAT WE THROW AWAY THE KEY. FOR THE FIRST THIRTY DAYS OF THEIR INCARCERATION, THE KKK KOOKS CAN USE THEIR ROBES FOR TOILET PAPER.

PARENTS WHO RAISE THEIR CHILDREN IN A HATE PREACHING ENVIRONMENT FORFEIT THE RIGHT TO RAISE THEM. THE KIDS WILL BE REMOVED AND PLACED IN A MORE NURTURING HOME. THE PARENT(S) IN RESIDENCE WILL BE STERILIZED. THEIR ASSETS WILL BE USED TO DEFRAY THE COST OF CHILD RELOCATION AND/OR THE SURGICAL PROCEDURE.

THERE WILL BE NO MORE FLYING OF THE CONFEDERATE FLAG. THE ARGUMENT THAT IT SYMBOLIZES SOME KIND OF RIGHTEOUS CHAPTER IN AMERICAN HISTORY IS ASININE.

THE WHOLE POINT TO THIS PROGRAM IS THAT IT IS OBVIOUS THAT WE CANNOT SOON DO AWAY WITH THOSE TELL TALE PHYSICAL DIFFERENCES WHICH HAVE DONE THEIR BEST TO HAUNT US DURING OUR RELATIVELY SHORT TIME ON EARTH. ONLY THROUGH INTERMARRIAGE AND ENLIGHTENMENT WILL THOSE DIFFERENCES CEASE TO EXIST. WHAT WE CAN DO IN THE INTERIM IS MAKE IT REAL UNCOMFORTABLE FOR THOSE WHO ESPOUSE RACIAL HATRED AND PREJUDICE. FREE SPEECH HAD AN ENTIRELY DIFFERENT MEANING OVER TWO HUNDRED YEARS AGO.

THE EASY THING FOR A FLEDGLING SPECIES IS TO BLAME A FAILED SYSTEM OR INEQUITABLE ECONOMY ON ANOTHER PERSON WHO HAPPENS THROUGH NO CHOICE OF HIS/HER OWN TO LOOK OR SPEAK DIFFERENTLY. THAT IS WHY IT IS IMPERATIVE TO

OVERCOMPENSATE IN SOME AREAS NOW IN AN EFFORT TO ACHIEVE EVENTUAL BALANCE. THE SCAPE GOATING HAS GOT TO STOP.

WE MUST NEVER AGAIN ALLOW TO HAPPEN IN THE UNITED STATES WHAT DID DURING WORLD WAR 11. ON APRIL 1ST, 1942, THE OFFICIAL AMERICAN POLICY OF JAPANESE INTERNMENT BEGAN. OVER 100,000 AMERICANS CITIZENS OF JAPANESE DESCENT WERE LOCKED UP AND BURGLARIZED. TO THEIR CREDIT, A SURPRISING NUMBER OF THE VICTIMS MANAGED TO RECOVER AND CONTRIBUTE, MOST EVIDENT BEING THE FAMOUS ALL JAPANESE 442 FIGHTERS.

ANOTHER INSIDIOUS ASPECT TO THE ISSUE IS THE PRESENCE OF WAGE AND GENERAL WORKPLACE DISCRIMINATION ALL ACROSS AMERICA. NOWHERE WAS IT MORE EVIDENT IN RECENT HISTORY THAN DURING THE FARM WORKERS STRUGGLE IN CALIFORNIA. IT DOESN'T REALLY MATTER THAT THE GOLDEN STATE USED TO BE PART OF MEXICO; THAT'S ANOTHER BOOK.

THE POOR FOLKS FINALLY GOT THE AGRICULTURE LABOR RELATIONS ACT PASSED IN 1967 ONLY TO HAVE THAT DIPSHIT DUKMEJIAN PRACTICALLY KILL IT LESS THAN TWENTY YEARS LATER.

SOMEHOW IT ALL SEEMS TO GET REDUCED TO ITS SIMPLEST TERMS. FOR ALL INTENTS AND PURPOSES, NATIVE AMERICANS HAVE LOST EVERYTHING. NOW THE ONLY REMINDER OF THE FREEDOM OF MOVEMENT THEY ONCE ENJOYED AS A BIRTHRIGHT CAN BE SEEN FROM A ROADSIDE STAND ON THE OUTSKIRTS OF THEIR RESERVATION AS A WINNEBAGO RV ROLLS BY.

THE UNITED STATES WAS RESPONSIBLE FOR LESS THAN 5% OF ALL SLAVERY. AFRICA AND EUROPE WERE THE PRINCIPLE PRACTITIONERS OF THAT BARBARIC TRADE.

THE UNITED STATES IS THE ONLY COUNTRY THAT FOUGHT A WAR TO END SLAVERY. OVER 600,000 MEN GAVE THEIR LIVES TO MANDATE FREEDOM FOR ALL SLAVES. REPARATIONS HAVE BEEN MADE WITH THE BLOOD OF WHITE MEN AND WOMEN WHO FOUGHT IN THE CIVIL WAR AND LATER, MARCHED IN THE SOUTH DURING THE MOVEMENT.

[This is being written in November of 2003. The subject is Native American Gaming. Having been responsible for the construction of two of the facilities, I have been unable to avoid some of the glaring realities inherent in Indian Gaming.

There is no defined protocol establishing rules that would govern the process by which "Trust" is established. Often as not, a BIA bureaucrat usually with a title such as Associate Solicitor General will provide a favorable opinion for money.

The lack of orthodox scrutiny (County building departments, Health Departments, State environmental agencies, etc) is an invitation to corporate crooks and thieves. I am currently attempting to help some 35 contractors recover $16 million dollars owed them for work completed and accepted. The fact that there are no defined rules makes the task extraordinarily difficult.

Sadder still is the conduct of some of the Tribes, not all; some.

Unscrupulous individuals will usurp the power and then kick legitimate Tribal members out, thereby keeping the money for themselves. While so doing, some will declare to the Federal Government that the ostracized members remain in good standing and keep the subsidies for health, education, and housing. Hopefully our efforts will force change.]

Taxes and the Economy

"A one time 100% deduction will be allowed the family of a deceased person who chose to be cremated as opposed to being buried in a grave that no one visits"

Somewhere in the Constitution of the United States of America, something was said about taxes being voluntary. I suppose that I could look it up but what would be the point? The only reason that language was used was to provide an out for any of the landed gentry. All the loopholes and/or deductions afforded the wealthy in America indicate that the original intent remains uncompromised. In fact those who occupy the upper echelons of income rarely pay any taxes at all.

The burden then falls upon the middle class and the poor to finance government, a structure that has become an obese, pulsating, convoluted, and cumbersome skeletal-less organism.

Meanwhile, the Internal Revenue Service has grown into some gargantuan, amorphous, quivering, and incompetent repository, relying on unsupervised and poorly trained personnel to fairly assess all the money from the masses. The worksheets and forms are long and complicated and the process is anything but fair.

Several things have to happen.

Taxes:

All individuals and corporations with incomes over twenty five thousand dollars annually should pay taxes. Ninety nine per cent of all exemptions should be eliminated including most standard deductions for single or married people. Every American should receive the same standard deduction regardless of marital status. Equity needs to be reinstated between the benefits given all taxpayers.

SOME DEPRECIATION SHOULD BE ALLOWED FOR INDIVIDUAL AND CORPORATE HARD GOODS SUCH AS VEHICLES AND EQUIPMENT. CATASTROPHIC HEALTH COSTS SHOULD ALSO BE DEDUCTIBLE.

THE ONLY OTHER ACCEPTABLE EXEMPTION FOR AN INDIVIDUAL OR BUSINESS SHOULD BE CHARITABLE, THAT IS, IF THEY CAN PROVE THAT THEY HAVE DONATED MONEY DIRECTLY TO THOSE IN NEED AS OPPOSED TO AN ADMINISTRATION (CONSIDER THE RECENT UNITED WAY SCANDAL), THAN THAT DOLLAR AMOUNT CAN BE CREDITED TOWARD THEIR TAX LIABILITY.

IT MUST BE NOTED THAT THERE EXISTS AN ENORMOUS DIFFERENCE IN FOCUS AND INTENT BETWEEN THE BILLIONAIRE WHO DONATES A HUNDRED MILLION DOLLARS TO AN INSTITUTION, HAS HIS NAME CONDITIONALLY IMMORTALIZED ON A NEW BUILDING, AND WRITES IT ALL OFF ON TAXES, AND THE PERSON WHO HAS A BUCK IN THEIR POCKET AND GIVES FIFTY CENTS TO A STRANGER. WHICH ACTION CONFORMS TO THE TRUE DEFINITION OF CHARITY?

POLITICAL ASPIRANTS SUCH AS THIS FORBES FELLOW WHO PROMOTES AN ACROSS THE BOARD SEVENTEEN PER CENT TAX FOR EVERYONE ARE MERELY SUBSTITUTING ONE INEQUITABLE SYSTEM FOR ANOTHER, BUT THEN OF COURSE HE'S A REPUBLICAN AND THEY CREATED BOTH. EVEN AN IDIOT CAN CALCULATE THAT THE POOR AND MIDDLE CLASS WOULD CONTINUE TO PAY MORE OF THEIR INCOME TO THE GOVERNMENT WITH A SINGLE FIGURE SYSTEM. THE FOLLOWING IS AN EXAMPLE OF HOW IT SHOULD BE.

- ANYONE EARNING LESS THAN TWENTY FIVE THOUSAND DOLLARS ANNUALLY SHOULD PAY NO TAX.

- THOSE EARNING TWENTY FIVE TO THIRTY THOUSAND SHOULD PAY FIVE PER CENT TAX ON THEIR INCOME.

- THIRTY TO THIRTY FIVE THOUSAND SHOULD PAY SEVEN AND ONE HALF PER CENT TAX ON THEIR TOTAL INCOME.

- THIRTY FIVE TO FORTY FIVE THOUSAND SHOULD PAY A TEN PER CENT TAX.

- Forty five thousand to fifty five thousand should pay a twelve and one half per cent tax.

- Fifty five thousand to seventy thousand should pay a fifteen per cent tax.

- Seventy to eighty thousand should pay a sixteen and one half per cent tax.

- Eighty to ninety thousand should pay an eighteen per cent tax.

- Ninety to one hundred thousand should pay a twenty per cent tax.

- One hundred to one hundred and twenty five thousand should pay a twenty two and one half per cent tax.

- All income over one hundred and twenty five thousand should be taxed twenty five percent. (2400 Americans with incomes exceeding $200,000 paid not a penny of tax in 1996)

Additionally, all second homes costing over one million dollars, plus all boats or planes costing over three hundred and fifty thousand dollars should be subject to a ten per cent luxury tax.

Corporations should not be allowed to take their famous "one time charges" because of incompetence, or allowed to write off any aspect of their mergers, or allowed to depreciate any of their buildings or equipment (regular citizens can't), or receive tax breaks or incentives for doing something they should have been doing all along (like installing safety and health apparati).

Couples with incomes under sixty thousand dollars should be allowed the existing deductions for children. Couples with incomes from sixty to one hundred thousand dollars annually should receive half the deductions

ABOVE. COUPLES ABOVE ONE HUNDRED THOUSAND DOLLARS IN ANNUAL INCOME ARE ON THEIR OWN.

ARTS:

NO PUBLIC MONEY WILL BE SPENT ON PERFORMANCE ART SUCH AS THE BALLET OR THE SYMPHONY. WEALTHY PATRONS ARE PERFECTLY CAPABLE OF SUPPORTING THOSE TYPES OF ACTIVITIES. PUBLIC MONEY SHOULD COMPREHENSIVELY BE SPENT ON COMMUNITY ART OF ALL KINDS.

THAT SUPPORT SHOULD INCLUDE THE ACQUISITION OF CENTERS, ART SUPPLIES, INSTRUCTION, AND COMMUNITY EXPOSURE PROGRAMS. THE ASSISTANCE SHOULD BE ALL ENCOMPASSING, AND INCLUDE NOT ONLY PHYSICAL MANIFESTATIONS SUCH AS SCULPTURE, AND PAINTING, BUT DANCE, THEATRE, WRITING, ALONG WITH ANY OTHER KIND OF CREATIVE ACTIVITY THAT EXPRESSES THE CULTURE OF THAT RESPECTIVE LOCALE.

ATTORNEY'S FEES:

THEIR WILL BE NO MORE WRITE OFFS OR DEDUCTIONS FOR ATTORNEY'S FEES RELATIVE TO BUSINESS. THE LOSER IN ANY LITIGATION, PERSONAL OR BUSINESS RELATED, WILL BE REQUIRED TO PAY ATTORNEY'S FEES FOR BOTH THE PLAINTIFF AND DEFENSE.

BANKS:

BANKS SHOULD PROHIBITED FROM CHARGING ANY MONEY WHATSOEVER FOR ATM TRANSACTIONS.

BANKS SHOULD BE ONLY ALLOWED TO CHARGE $10.00 OR LESS FOR CHECKS WITH INSUFFICIENT FUNDS.

ANY TIME THAT BANKS ARE CONDUCTING ANY KIND OF ACTIVITY THAT INVOLVES CHECKING, THEY MUST KEEP THEIR DOORS OPEN FOR BUSINESS. FOR EXAMPLE, IF A BANK IS INVOLVED IN ANY TYPE OF FINANCIAL PROCEDURE DIRECTLY RELATED TO CUSTOMER'S CHECKING ACCOUNTS, THEY MUST ALLOW THE CUSTOMERS ACCESS TO THE BUSINESS. THEIR FAILURE TO DO SO NOW PAYS BIG DIVIDENDS IN TERMS OF BAD CHECK CHARGES.

THE PRIME INTEREST RATE FOR BUSINESS MUST BE AVAILABLE TO THE GENERAL PUBLIC.

CHURCHES:

CHURCHES IN AMERICA ARE NOTHING MORE THAN BUSINESSES. THEY OWN REAL ESTATE, STOCKS, AND APPARENTLY A LOCK ON TAX EXEMPTION. THAT HAS TO CHANGE.

THE LOCATION AND FINANCIAL HEALTH OF CHURCHES, MIRRORS THAT OF SOCIETY AT LARGE. MOST OF THE PRIME REAL ESTATE IN AMERICA IS OWNED BY EITHER THE MILITARY OR RELIGIOUS ORGANIZATIONS. THE MILITARY ASIDE, THERE IS NO JUSTIFICATION FOR TAX EXEMPT STATUS BEING GRANTED TO CHURCHES AND THEIR SATELLITES WHO CONTRIBUTE NOTHING TO THE WELFARE OF THEIR PARISHIONERS.

UNLIKE A PUBLIC UTILITY THAT OFTEN IS ALLOWED THE SIX PER CENT PROFIT (WHICH IS USUALLY CLOSER TO SIXTY), CHURCHES SHOULD MAKE NO PROFIT WHATSOEVER.

FOR TAX PURPOSES, CHURCHES SHOULD BE REQUIRED TO FILE A SPECIFIC FINANCIAL STATEMENT LISTING THEIR EXPENDITURES (INCLUDING MAINTENANCE OF REAL PROPERTY I.E.: BUILDINGS, VEHICLES, ETC.) ALONG WITH REVENUES. IF REVENUES EXCEED EXPENDITURES, THE DIFFERENCE WILL BE THE AMOUNT OF THEIR TAX. IF THE CHURCH CAN DOCUMENT CHARITABLE CONTRIBUTIONS SUCH AS SOUP KITCHENS, CLOTHING, HOUSING, EDUCATION, ETC., THE DOLLAR AMOUNT OF THAT ACTIVITY CAN BE USED TO DEFRAY TAXES. ACCEPTABLE EXEMPTIONS WILL NOT BE STOCK OR LAND ACQUISITIONS, OR NEW FURNITURE FOR THE PASTOR'S OFFICE. THE CHURCHES WILL ALSO USE THE SAME FORMULA WHEN CALCULATING THEIR PROPERTY TAX; AND ALL CHURCH PROPERTY WILL BE TAXED.

HYPOTHETICALLY, IF THE CATHOLIC CHURCH IN AMERICA HAD A COMBINED TAX BITE OF FIFTY MILLION DOLLARS, ALL THEY WOULD HAVE TO DO TO AVOID PAYMENT IS TO CONTRIBUTE OR DONATE REAL GOODS OR SERVICES IN THAT AMOUNT. WHY, THAT WOULD ALMOST BE A MIRACLE.

COLD WAR AND USSR'S ECONOMIC COLLAPSE:

FOR THE RECORD: TRICKY DICK NIXON HAD NO MORE TO DO WITH ENDING THE "COLD WAR" THAN REAGAN HAD TO DO WITH THE COLLAPSE OF RUSSIA'S ECONOMY. THE TWO EVENTS SIMPLY HAPPENED TO OCCUR DURING THEIR RESPECTIVE PRESIDENCIES AND HAD NOTHING TO DO WITH THEIR INFLUENCE OR EXPERTISE. ON THE CONTRARY, HAD WE BEEN FORTUNATE ENOUGH TO HAVE HAD SITTING ENLIGHTENED AND VISIONARY "LEADERS", BOTH HISTORICAL OCCASIONS WOULD HAVE PASSED YEARS EARLIER THUS ACCELERATING AT LEAST A SMALL PART OF PROGRESS TOWARD PEACE.

CREDIT CARDS:

CREDIT CARD INTEREST RATES CAN NO LONGER EXCEED SIXTEEN PER CENT ANNUALLY.

IF A CREDIT CARD COMPANY SENDS A PRE APPROVED SOLICITATION WITH A GUARANTEED LINE OF CREDIT TO ANY AMERICAN CITIZEN, THE CARD COMPANY HAS TO HONOR THEIR OFFER.

CREMATION:

IN DEATH, ALL WE ESSENTIALLY DO IS SHED OUR SKINS, THEN CONTINUE ON WITH OUR SOUL'S JOURNEY. WE ARE ALL INDEED ACTORS ON A STAGE WITH MANY SETS, PERFORMING AN ETERNAL PLAY.

A ONE TIME 100% DEDUCTION WILL BE ALLOWED THE FAMILY OF A DECEASED PERSON WHO CHOSE TO BE CREMATED AS OPPOSED TO BEING BURIED IN A GRAVE THAT NO ONE VISITS.

FEDERAL RESERVE BOARD:

THE FEDERAL RESERVE BOARD SHOULD BE DISBANDED IMMEDIATELY. IT IS ABSOLUTELY PREPOSTEROUS THAT ANY GROUP OF INDIVIDUALS OR A PERSON HAVE THE KIND OF INFLUENCE OVER

A NATION'S ECONOMY THAT ALAN GREENSPAN AND HIS CRONIES ENJOY.

ALL THE FRB DOES IS PROTECT BIG BUSINESS AND RESTRICT THE POOR. HERE IN SIMPLE TERMS IS HOW IT WORKS.

BUSINESS HAS ALWAYS BEEN OFFERED LOWER INTEREST RATES THAN ANY PRIVATE CITIZEN ON ANY TYPE OF LOAN DESPITE THE FACT THAT BUSINESS FAILURES PROPORTIONATELY OUT NUMBER PERSONAL BANKRUPTCIES.

LOW UNEMPLOYMENT COMBINED WITH HIGH WAGES THREATENS THE PRIVILEGED FINANCIAL POSITION OF BIG BUSINESS AND CORPORATE INTERESTS. THE MORE PEOPLE THAT HAVE MONEY, THE MORE MONEY THAT WILL BE SPENT, NECESSITATING AN INCREASE IN BUSINESS INVENTORIES AND/OR PLANT EXPANSION. IDEALLY, A BUSINESS WOULD WANT TO BORROW AT THE LOWEST RATE OF INTEREST POSSIBLE, AS WOULD ANY CITIZEN. WITH PROSPERITY COMES INFLATION (REAL OR IMAGINED) AND INTEREST RATES WILL BE RAISED TO SLOW GROWTH, OR IN OTHER WORDS, TO RAISE UNEMPLOYMENT AND DROP WAGES. WHAT DOES THAT REALLY DO?

BUSINESSES WILL LAY OFF WORKERS. THEY WILL ALLOW THEIR INVENTORIES TO RUN LOW AND WILL DELAY EXPANSION. AS A CONSEQUENCE OF REDUCED EXPENDITURES, CEO'S AND THEIR ILK WILL GRANT THEMSELVES HUGE BONUSES AND PAY INCREASED DIVIDENDS TO THEIR SHAREHOLDERS.

IT MEANS THAT JOHN Q. PUBLIC WILL HAVE TO POSTPONE BUYING THAT FIRST HOME OR PUT OFF BUYING THAT NEW CAR. IT MEANS THAT THE COLLEGE OF CHOICE FOR THE HIGH SCHOOL GRAD MAY NO LONGER BE AFFORDABLE. IT ALSO MEANS THAT AS THE ECONOMY SLOWS, INTEREST RATES WILL DROP. BIG BUSINESS WILL ONCE AGAIN HAVE ACCESS TO CHEAP MONEY WHILE THE MASSES BUSY THEMSELVES ADJUSTING TO THE ARTIFICIAL ECONOMIC CHAOS IMPOSED ON THEM BY GREENSPAN AND HIS GOONS.

BY THE TIME THE DUST HAS SETTLED, BUSINESS WILL HAVE MADE A BUNDLE THROUGH THE RIPPLE EFFECT THROUGHOUT THE

David Hayden

ECONOMY, AND THE CYCLE OF CITIZEN MANIPULATION WILL BE READY TO BEGIN AGAIN.

The new and far simpler tax structure, along with the absence of loopholes and write offs, the increase in the minimum wage, and the health care requirements for employers, will go a long way toward "leveling the playing field" one of another of the latest in 90's buzz words or terms.

Foreign Aid:

No more money will be sent to any non Democratic country for assistance for any reason. If some kind of humanitarian effort is essential, the United States Government should send the personnel and supplies necessary to accomplish the mission. We will build the dams, schools, roads, etc. rather than continue to waste money in the deep pockets of the corrupt Dictators and politicos.

Accordingly, the agency referred to as Aid to International Development will cease to exist. If there ever was an example of a government agency out of control, this is such a beast. Elephants are considered by most thoughtful and concerned people to be endangered. To deny that these intelligent and ancient animals have been the victim of a form of genocide is to assume all's right with the world. Our fearless administrator of AID is currently sending 21 million taxpayer dollars to Africa to promote tourism by hunting Elephants. I say we ought to hunt the person in charge of AID.

Foreign Trade:

American companies (as well as foreign) that utilize slave or sweat shop labor in the manufacture of their products beyond the borders of the United States will not be allowed to import or sell those goods domestically. All tax exemptions or deductions for which they might have been eligible will be eliminated.

Business interests from America that operate in, negotiate with, or produce goods in countries that practice human rights and/or animal rights abuses will not be allowed to import or sell their product(s) in the United States. Moreover, if the parent company resides in America while the above is occurring, they would be subject to fines exceeding one half of their actual/real value.

There will be no parts of any animal's body imported into the United States i.e. furs, ivory, horns, fins, testicles, etc. Violators will lose their citizenship and be deported following seizure of all of their assets.

Minimum Wage:

The minimum wage should be raised to ten dollars an hour immediately.

Ranching:

There will be no "ranching" or raising of Alligators, Ostriches, Lions, or other previously considered non edible animals in the U.S. for food purposes. Veal or any other young animal from any species can no longer be used to appease the appetites of the insensitive and unenlightened carnivores in the country. The method used to "grow" the animals redefines cruelty.

Stocks:

It is virtually impossible to prevent insider trading, however one thorn in the side of every non industry connected investor can be eliminated.

All Initial Public Offerings (IPO) should be published in the business sections of all newspapers at least two weeks in advance of the event and have available for purchase a minimum of 95% of the stock.

DAVID HAYDEN

WELFARE

"PEOPLE IN THE SECOND HALF OF THE TWENTIETH CENTURY HAVE BEEN SO CAUGHT UP IN THEIR PERSONAL QUESTS THAT THEY'VE LOST SIGHT OF THE FACT THAT AS ALL GO, SO GOES ONE"

FROM THE 1951 EDITION OF WEBSTER'S DICTIONARY, 1. WELFARE: EXEMPTION FROM MISFORTUNE, SICKNESS, CALAMITY, OR EVIL; THE ENJOYMENT OF HEALTH AND THE <u>COMMON</u> BLESSINGS OF LIFE; PROSPERITY; HAPPINESS; WELL BEING 2. A BLESSING

THE COMMON BLESSINGS OF LIFE; TO PARAPHRASE WHAT HEMINGWAY SAID IN HIS LAST LINE IN "THE SUN ALSO RISES", "WOULDN'T IT BE PRETTY TO THINK SO".

PEOPLE IN THE SECOND HALF OF THE TWENTIETH CENTURY HAVE BEEN SO CAUGHT UP IN THEIR PERSONAL QUESTS THAT THEY'VE LOST SIGHT OF THE FACT THAT AS ALL GO, SO GOES ONE.

IT'S THE OLD CASTLE AND MOAT CONCEPT; GREAT WEALTH AMASSED BY SO FEW AT THE EXPENSE OF SO MANY. IF ANY TRUTH IS EVIDENT FROM THAT DYNAMIC IT IS THAT THE SECURITY OF THE FEW IS IMAGINED AND SHORT LIVED FROM A HISTORICAL PERSPECTIVE. THEY'VE ALL FALLEN, ALL THE GREAT CIVILIZATIONS, CULTURES, AND SOCIETIES. EVERY REASON FANCIED HAS BEEN PROFFERED FOR THEIR COLLAPSE, CONQUEST, DISEASE, NATURAL CATASTROPHE, ETC., BUT NONE ADDRESS THE CENTRAL CAUSE.

MOST OF MANKIND FINDS IT VIRTUALLY IMPOSSIBLE TO LINK IN REAL TERMS THE WELFARE OF ALL LIVING THINGS. THERE IS NO UNDERSTANDING OF THE SYMBIOTIC RELATIONSHIP AMONG ALL LIFE FORMS AS INTENDED BY OUR CREATOR.

THE REAL TRUTH IS THAT IN INCREASING NUMBERS, PEOPLE ARE NO LONGER GOING TO FIT IN THE MAINSTREAM OF SOCIETY FOR THE SIMPLE REASON THAT PEOPLE WILL NO LONGER BE PARTICIPANTS IN THE PROCESS. COMPUTER DRIVEN AUTOMATION WILL CONTROL MUCH OF THE MANUFACTURING OF GOODS. PEOPLE WILL SPEND

MORE TIME IN THEIR HOMES FROM WHERE THEY WILL WORK, SHOP, AND BE ENTERTAINED.

THEY WILL BE THE LUCKY ONES AND EVENTUALLY, THE FORTUNATE FEW. WITH EACH PASSING YEAR MORE RESOURCES IN TERMS OF TIME AND MONEY WILL HAVE TO BE DIRECTED TO ASSIST THOSE FOLKS WHO NEVER HAD A SHOT AT THE RAPIDLY DISAPPEARING OPPORTUNITY THAT EXISTED IN THE FIRST HALF OF THE 1900's. IT IS ESSENTIAL THAT WE REFINE AND STREAMLINE OUR WELFARE SYSTEM TO MEET FUTURE NEEDS.

NO MATTER HOW HIGH TECH AMERICA BECOMES, WE MUST INSIST THAT WE PROVIDE ALL OF OUR CITIZENS AT LEAST THE ESSENTIAL FIVE, HOUSING, EDUCATION, CLOTHING, NUTRITION, AND HEALTH CARE. THOSE OF US, WHO THROUGH GOOD FORTUNE OR FATE HAVE MANAGED TO CARRY OUR WEIGHT, DON'T NEED TO RANT AND RAVE ABOUT WELFARE ABUSE AND WASTE. WHAT WE ALL DO NEED TO DO IS TO DISCOVER WAYS TO CREATIVELY INCLUDE THOSE LESS FORTUNATE IN THE EVER CHANGING FOLD. ABUSES WILL ALWAYS EXIST IN EVERY ASPECT OF SOCIETY. THAT KIND OF BEHAVIOR HAS NOTHING TO DO WITH THE COLOR OF A PERSON'S SKIN; IT MERELY IS WHAT SHOULD BE AN ANTICIPATED RESPONSE BY A PRIMITIVE SPECIES OF ANIMAL.

DREAMS CHANGE. THEY RESPOND TO THEIR ENVIRONMENTS. THE KEY IS TO KEEP THEM POSITIVE AND RESPONSIVE TO REAL NEED.

CONCLUSION

NOTHING HAS REALLY CHANGED SINCE THE ANCIENT FEUDAL DAYS. WE STILL HAVE THE LORDS AND SERFS ALTHOUGH THE NAMES HAVE CHANGED. THEY ARE NOW CEO'S AND SENATORS, SUPREME COURTS AND CREDIT CARD COMPANIES.

THE OPERATIVE BUZZ WORDS HAVE BECOME "EMPOWERMENT' AND "SELF ESTEEM" REPLACING THE OLD "INTEGRITY", "HONOR", AND "FIDELITY". FORTUNE IS NO LONGER FOUND IN FRIENDSHIP BUT IN A FORTUNE 500 COMPANY. WE ARE ENCOURAGED TO ASSERT OUR INDEPENDENCE YET ARE FORCED BY FASHION TO DRESS AND ACT ALIKE. MADISON AVENUE PROMOTES THE "LOOK" KNOWING FULL WELL THAT FOR MOST IT IS IMPOSSIBLE TO ACHIEVE. MANY OF OUR YOUTH HAVE NO FUNCTIONAL FAMILY, LITTLE OR NO SUCCESS IN SCHOOL, AND NO FUTURE AS AN ADULT IN A RAPIDLY DISINTEGRATING SOCIETY. MOM AND POP STORES HAVE BEEN REPLACED BY CHAINS. GENERAL PRACTITIONERS AND HOUSE CALLS HAVE BEEN REPLACED BY HMO'S AND THE ONLY WORK AVAILABLE IS NOW IN SALES OR ON ASSEMBLY LINES.

EVERYTHING IS TOPSY TURVY. AMERICANS IN THE ARROGANCE REFER TO EARLIER AND OFTEN ANCIENT CULTURES IN OTHER COUNTRIES AS THIRD WORLD. THIS IMPRESSION IS BASED IN LARGE MEASURE BECAUSE THEY DON'T USE "VELCRO" OR "TEFLON", BECAUSE THEY DO ENJOY A CLOSE AND SYMBIOTIC RELATIONSHIP WITH MOTHER EARTH AS OPPOSED TO OUR ADVERSARIAL STANCE, AND BECAUSE WE, AS CONSTANT HOSTAGES OF OUR STRUGGLE FOR SURVIVAL, DO NOT UNDERSTAND THEM.

WE IN FACT ARE THE THIRD WORLD COUNTRY; THEY THE FIRST.

THE REAL PROBLEM IS WITH OUR COLLECTIVE PERCEPTION OF THE EVENTS THAT ULTIMATELY COMPRISE HISTORY. HISTORY FOR ALL INTENTS AND PURPOSES "SPRINGS ETERNAL". WE CONVERSELY LIVE RELATIVELY SHORT LIVES, ONE AT A TIME. THEREFORE, WHILE ACTING AS APPRENTICE ACADEMICS WE CEREBRALLY COMPREHEND OUR IMPACT ON THE PLANET; WE FAIL TO FEEL THAT INFLUENCE ON A DAILY BASIS. CONSEQUENTLY, AS A SPECIES, THE LONG TERM IMPACT OF OUR PRESENCE ON EARTH

GOES LARGELY UNNOTICED AND UNCHANGED UNTIL IT IS TOO LATE. IT IS "THE UNTIL IT'S TOO LATE" FOR ALL LIVING THINGS ISSUE THAT THIS BOOK IS ABOUT.

OUR FORTUNATE FEW, THE AFFLUENT, SPEND THEIR TIME AND MONEY PURSUING "NEW AGE" METHODS OF PERSONAL GROWTH AND ENLIGHTENMENT WITHOUT ACKNOWLEDGING THEIR ANTIQUE ROOTS.

WE EXPORT OUR HIGH TECH MEANS OF MASS DESTRUCTION IN THE FORM OF MILITARY WEAPONS, MINING, LOGGING, OIL DRILLING EQUIPMENT, AND EXPERTISE WHILE COMPENSATING FOR SHRINKING MARKETS IN TOBACCO BY SHIPPING THE CANCER STICKS OVERSEAS.

THE TEARS WE SHED EULOGIZING THE DEATH OF A DREAM EVAPORATE QUIETLY INTO OBLIVION.

THE LOSS OF OUR COLLECTIVE LIGHT THROUGH SENSORY TRAUMA IS CAUSING A TOTAL COLLAPSE OF THE SUN; CREATING A COURSE THAT APPEARS TO HAVE US ALL JUMPING OFF THE EDGE OF NIGHT AND LANDING ON THE DARK SIDE OF THE DAY.

WE NEED TO ADOPT AND USE SOME OF THESE AGGRESSIVE SOLUTIONS IF WE EVER HOPE TO HAVE BEEN PART OF PERIOD IN TIME WHEN HOMO SAPIENS COULD CALL THEMSELVES SOMETHING OTHER THAN A FEW BRIGHT LIGHTS IN A WORLD FULL OF DIMLY LIT BULBS.

ABOUT THE AUTHOR

DAVID AND HIS TWIN KATIE WERE BORN IN RIVERSIDE, CALIFORNIA, 1945. HE DROPPED OUT OF HIGH SCHOOL IN 1962 AND ENLISTED IN THE MARINE CORPS. DAVID RECEIVED HIS AA FROM MONTEREY JUNIOR COLLEGE IN 1967 AND HIS BA FROM SONOMA STATE COLLEGE IN 1970. HE HAD NO CHILDREN BY CHOICE. DAVID LIVED, WITHOUT RETURNING, ON MAUI FROM 1978 UNTIL 1990. HE WAS PASSIONATELY INVOLVED IN NATIVE HAWAIIAN RIGHTS AS WELL AS OUTRIGGER CANOE PADDLING. DAVID FORMED "WHALE AID" IN 1988. HE ALSO RODE BAREBACK IN THE PRCA AND PLAYED RUGBY WITH HIS MATES IN NO. CALIFORNIA. HE HAS WORKED IN CONSTRUCTION MOST OF HIS LIFE HAVING RECENTLY COMPLETED A NATIVE AMERICAN CASINO IN THE YOSEMITE HILLS EAST OF FRESNO. DAVID LIVES WITH HIS SWEETHEART TAMMY IN OAKHURST, CA. HE HAS WRITTEN A NOVEL "ONE PADDLE, ONE SUN" AND AN EXTENSIVE COLLECTION OF POETRY AND SONGS.